Lust and Grace

Lust and Grace

Volume 1

Sex and Eroticism in the Works of Muslim Scholars

Ali Ghandour

Translated by
Margarita Giovanni

Editio Gryphus

Original title, published in German: *Lust und Gunst: Sex und Erotik bei den muslimischen Gelehrten*, 2015.

This publication has been typeset in Vollkorn, designed by Friedrich Althausen and Adobe's Source Sans Pro.

A catalogue record for this book is available from the German Library. http://dnb.dnb.de

ISBN: 978-3-9817551-4-5

Printed and bound by Ingram Spark, USA.

Contents

بسم الله الرحمن الرحيم
الحمد لله والصلاة والسلام على خير خلق الله وعلى آله وصحبه

Prefaces

"*Blessed is He who beautified the woman with clitoral prepuce and buttocks.*"[1] With these words, Imam as-Suyūṭī (d. 1505) started one of his many books on sex. Why didn't he need to justify himself; and, why is a statement like this considered to be heretical today? These two questions could summarize the entire discourse on sex, intimacy and eroticism in most Muslim societies of our time. About seventeen years ago, I discovered the book *Rugū'aš-šayḫ ilā ṣibāh fī al-quwwati 'alā al-bāh* (The old man's return to the power of his teenage years) by the famous Ottoman scholar Imam Ibn Kamāl Pascha (d. 1534) in my father's library. In my "secret" readings back then, the book kept on shocking me, because it related almost everything that is taboo for most Muslims today, namely the intimate description of the male and female body up to the most frivolous stories. The protagonists were all sorts of people in society: scholars, rulers, God's servants and prostitutes. From the study of this book during my adolescence, I learned about the various aspects of sex. It is something controversial in itself when a teenager, like me, gets his first sex education from a Muslim scholar who died about 450 years ago and particularly if this happens at a time when the same topic, namely sex, is tabooed in the name of Islam. This is why the research of this subject acts as a mirror which shows us the drastic changes in understanding religion over the last two hundred years. And, no other topic conveys the contrast between the understanding of Islam before and after the 19th century so drastically.

The publication series "Lust and Grace" examines the topic of sex and eroticism among Muslims from various perspectives and areas of life. The focus is on the premodern age, which in this context is the time before colonialism. The first volume "Sex and Eroticism in the Works of Muslim Scholars" presents the general relevance of this topic. God willing, further volumes will be published, including translations of classical texts as well as surveys on the subject.

Lust stands for the human being and her/his relationship to oneself as well as to other creatures. Grace, on the other hand, describes the relation between man and the Creator. The different types of God's grace towards the world includes lust as well. From this perspective, lust was and is understood as an act of God's mercy towards His creatures throughout this publication series and as an act of God's boon when lust is the subject of research. This concept of lust will become even more evident when one realizes that not only poets, doctors and narrators have written about this subject but also numerous theologians.

I am aware that this is a hot topic which might cause indignation or confusion, because today's picture of Islam, as well as the idea of a theologian many people have, does not comply with the facts discussed in this volume. This text shall inspire reflection. The many ideas about society, piety, shamefacedness, religiousness and Islam, which people usually have in mind, will be scrutinized here.

The idealization of history is nothing but an illusion. The more research is done on different aspects of Muslim's everyday life throughout history, the clearer becomes the image of societies in which all the aspects of human nature are present; they include lust, deceit, sorrow, envy, jocularity, idiocy as well as those properties which are beyond good and evil.

This study aims to provide insights and impressions from different epochs between the 7th and the 19th century; firstly as an illustration of the dynamics of Muslim societies in contrast to the wishful thinking that earlier Muslims led an ideal life; and, secondly as a way to deconstruct the image of an 'Islamic'[2] ideal. The search for this ideal keeps us from realizing the diversity and changes in life. It would therefore be wrong to wonder how far early concepts of Muslim scholars and Muslims in general had corresponded to such an ideal since it never existed. In reality, a series of ideals and discourses had developed and co-existed and they all successfully claimed to be part of Islam.

Anyone who wants to shape people – and thus society – into faultless beings, wants to correct God.

The scholars in the premodern age did not strive for a standardized society. This point is important to realize, because it explains aspects of scholars' attitudes towards various phenomena in society, which had also existed in their day. Otherwise, one will be stunned by their texts about pederasty or same-sex intercourse. Their thinking was characterized by pragmatics.

The studies in this work do not have any theologically normative character. So, the point is not assessing different practices but rather illustrating how Muslim scholars treat the topic in general.

Tradition in theological context means the entirety of discourses based on epistemological, ontological and normative premises of *kalām* (systematic theology), fiqh (science of deducing norms)[3] and *taṣawwuf* (science of inner mystical dimensions).[4]

Besides the essay, this first volume includes two excerpts from different classical works. The first excerpt, which was written by Imam Ibn al-ʿArabī (d. 1240), gives us an impression of eroticism in a Sufi context. The second text was written by the hadith scholar and ethicist Imam al-Ḫarāʾiṭī (d. 939). Its relevance lies in the numerous transmitted narratives and anecdotes from the first two centuries after Hegira which can serve as examples of several issues stated in the text.

Ali Ghandour
Hamburg, 2015

Our Lord is He who gave each thing its form and then guided. Q 20:50. *Sayyidunā Ibn ʿAbbās said: "This means: guided to sexual intercourse."*[5]

How would Muslims today respond if a Muslim scholar had written a Kama Sutra-like book or an erotic novel? The outcry would surely be huge. Today's refusal of such a book is based on its deviation from common modern thought patterns, which are nowadays regarded as essential elements of tradition all along. Such an angry reaction was seen clearly some years ago, when ʿAbd al-Bārī az-Zamzamī, a Moroccan mufti, declared in a radio broadcast that it is permissible for unmarried lascivious women to use carrots or sex toys for masturbation if they otherwise fear to commit adultery. For many Muslims, this fatwa was so strange and scandalous that it got its own label: the carrot-fatwa.[6] In media and social networks the fatwa was the subject of mockery and outrage.

Az-Zamzamī's position is not new at all, but rather people's reactions are. When it comes to the topic of sex, discrepancy is a typical feature. The opinion of az-Zamzamī is not innovative as Imam al-Ḥasan al-Baṣrī (d. 728)[7] had already stated that a woman who uses an object for sexual stimulation to satisfy her desire[8] does not undertake an act of sin.[9] The acceptance or rejection of such a position was discussed with serenity on the basis of fiqh without defaming

Imam al-Ḥasan al-Baṣrī as a person or labeling his position as perverse, shameless or the like.[10] It was just one opinion among many others.

The tabooing and scandalizing of sex and eroticism among the faithful today, if one tries to speak about it publicly, is by no means a matter that is rooted in tradition. On the contrary, this is a modern phenomenon which is mainly the result of adopting certain modern-age values and thought patterns, which are alien to the spirit of Islam, when examined more closely. The reasons behind this transformation in thinking and the ways in which this new kind of 'prudery' developed and spread among Muslims has been examined in other studies.[11] This book is rather addressing the question how Muslims in premodern age thought and wrote about the topic of sex and eroticism and what Muslim scholars wrote about it in particular. Later in Chapter III, the focus is on the works of the polymath Imam as-Suyūṭī, as one concrete example. Not because he is an exception but because in those days the amount of erotic writings and books which deal with the subject of sex is so huge that mentioning them all would go beyond the scope of this text.[12]

To begin with, it should be noted that the term 'sexuality' as a category has been avoided intentionally in this book, because sexuality as a construct and category represents a modern concept. People in Muslim societies in the particular geographical area this book refers to and the premodern era, which is understood as the time before the 19th century, knew sex but not sexuality.[13] Especially the isolation of sex into the category of sexuality, which became an object of research and created numerous definitions and categorizations that are scrutinized in detail and put in 'clear' terms, has nothing in common with the traditional Muslim view of sex and eroticism.

The erotic is as omnipresent in human existence and as diverse as the diversity of humans themselves, so that it cannot be brought together into one category. We encounter it in the Koran and in different chapters of fiqh. Eroticism and sex appear in hadith, in *taṣawwuf*, in poetry, in medicine, in humor, in everyday life and naturally at night.

The perception of the omnipresence and fluidity of this topic gave rise - as Foucault stated - to an *ars erotica* in premodern Muslim societies instead of a *scientia sexualis* as in the West.[14] This should be self-evident if Islam is to be understood as *dīn*, as a way of living, an attitude and a philosophy of life. If Islam is thought of in holistic terms, categories like sacred or profane do not make much sense, as the world is both, sacred in relation to its Creator and profane in its worldliness. Likewise, the Greek antagonism between the spiritual and the physical may have its foundation in ancient philosophies or in some religions, but not in

Islam. Because in Islam, the good is known by what we recognize as the True and by what brings us closer to the One within the framework of the Sharia,[15] be it mentally or physically.

To understand this point is crucial for comprehending the self-conception of the theology/ies of Islam concerning many topics, such as the question of ownership, marriage, or the physical pleasures in this world and the hereafter. Unlike in Christianity, sex in Islam has never been seen as something sinful or mean which should be avoided.[16]

This positive attitude towards life, to put it in the words of Nietzsche,[17] led to two completely different or even contrary ways of dealing with the sexual itself. Sex, as we will see later, has not been experienced as something purely physical but Muslims in premodern age also took its spiritual, erotic and social aspects into consideration. The Prophet ﷺ said: "*Three things of your world were made delightful to me: women, perfume and prayer.*"[18] In another transmission, he compared intercourse with charity, thus with a good deed which is loved by God[19] and Imam Ǧa'far aṣ-Ṣādiq[20] transmitted: "*The more faithful one becomes the more does increase his love for women.*"[21] He also said: "*The love for women is among the character traits of the Prophet.*"[22] These statements illustrate the open and positive attitude of the Prophet ﷺ towards this topic which influenced Muslims for a long time.

Since the beginning of Islam eroticism and sex have been an issue. God ﷻ Himself - even if only in some passages - states these issues in the Koran. The virgins in paradise, for example, are described precisely and their erotic aspects are stressed. Imam ar-Rāzī (d. 1209)[23] stated that the maidens of paradise were never designated by the genus name 'woman' but always by their handsome attributes.[24] Victorian prudery does not exist in the Koran. In the Koran, God ﷻ calls things as they are. So, He states about the women of paradise: *"and women, same-aged, with swelling breasts."* Q 78:33. Imam ar-Rāzī states about the word *qawāʿib*: *"These are bosomed [nawāhid] women, their breasts well-shaped [taka"abat] and bosomy [tafallakat]."*[25]

Another verse states: *"There are those who lower their gaze, untouched by man or jinn."* Q55:56; in this passage, the verb *ṭamaṯa* is used which implies both, the literal meaning 'to deflorate' as well as the allusive meaning of sexual intercourse or touching.[26] The already Germanized word '*Huri*' which appears in Q 44:54, Q 52:20 and Q 56:22 means 'the beautiful white young lady' or 'the black-eyed woman'.[27] The word *ḥūr* is connected with '*īn* which means a woman with beautiful and large eyes. While explaining the term *ʿīn*, Imam Ibn al-Qayyim (d. 1350)[28] did not miss the opportunity to make the reader believe that small eyes are among the flaws: "*rather smallness (narrowness) is praiseworthy in four limbs, that is the mouth, the ears, the nose and 'that'* [the vagina]."[29]

In Q 56:36-37, God describes the virgins of paradise as *'urub*, meaning the lovestruck, delightful, coquettish and alluring woman.[30] The discussion about the women of paradise offers the theologian two new insights. The first insight is a normative one, namely that sex is something praiseworthy and desirable, with which God actually rewards the believers. For this reason, sex must not be seen as something base or bad, as long as it is enjoyed and acted upon within permitted limits. The second insight is of a theological nature: the hereafter is not solely spiritual but it is also a sensual world with substance, space and time.[31]

Now we come to those Koranic parts which directly discuss sexual intercourse. One of the most famous verses in this context is Q 2:223: "*Your wives are a place of sowing of seed for you; so approach them where [annā,] you like.*" The preposition *annā*, which means 'where', 'how' and also 'when', was subject of an interesting discussion, because the permission of anal intercourse depends on the reading of this preposition. Today, many theologians, not to speak of ordinary Muslims, regard even speaking about such topics as perverse and shameless. If nowadays someone is told that a number of scholars considered anal intercourse permissible, their positions will most probably be regarded as scandalous.[32] A look at the works of earlier scholars reveal legal opinions like those of Imam Ibn Qudāma (d. 1223)[33], a prominent Hanbalite jurist, who wrote in his encyclopedia of law, *al-Muġnī*:

> *(the permission) of anal sex has been transmitted by Ibn 'Umar Zayd b. Aslam and Nāfi'. It is transmitted from Imam Mālik that he stated: 'I did not meet anybody I took as paradigm in my religion who doubted the permission (of anal intercourse).'*[34]

Ibn Qudāma himself maintained that the majority of scholars considered anal sex as prohibited. But his own conviction did not prevent him to mention other opinions as well, and name their representatives. The same applies to other scholars like for example Imam al-Qurṭubī (d. 1273):[35] Although he deemed anal sex as prohibited as did the majority of scholars,[36] he nevertheless mentioned those who regarded it permissible and among them are important imams of the 2nd and 3rd generation like Sa'īd b. al-Musayyib, Muḥammad b. Ka'b al-Quraẓī, 'Abd al-Malik b. al-Māğišūn[37] next to those already named before. This has been approved by Imam Abū Bakr Ibn al-'Arabī (d. 1148)[38] in his commentary *Aḥkām al-qur'ān* (The norms of the Koran):

> *The scholars have different judgments concerning the permission of anal intercourse. So, a large group allowed it. Ibn Šaʿbān collected (these opinions) in his book Ğimāʿ an-niswān wa-aḥkām al-qurʾān (sexual intercourse with women and the Koranic norms) and he attributed the opinion of permission (of anal intercourse) to a number of noble companions of the Prophet and their successors (at-tabiʿīn) [...].*[39]

al-Qāḍī Abū Bakr Ibn al-ʿArabī did not tell us his own view in this legal matter. He mentioned both opinions together without taking sides. But the fact that he starts with the opinion of those who regarded it permissible and strengthens their statement with phrases such as '*a large group*' or '*a noble group of companions of the Prophet and their successors*' might indicate which opinion he himself preferred. But far more important is the author's frankness. To mention both opinions of this current sensitive topic was unproblematic for him, because he did not experience this as a violation of modesty. For him, the question of anal intercourse was just one legal and exegetical question among others. In contrast, some scholars not only mentioned their points of view between the lines, but spoke quite frankly in favor of anal sex. Among these we find Imam Muḥyī ad-Dīn Ibn al-ʿArabī. In his commentary of the Koran *ʿAǧāʾib al-ʿirfān* (The wonders of knowledge), of which only one volume has survived, he wrote:

> *People hold different opinions regarding anal intercourse with a lawful woman. Some have allowed it and some have prohibited it. (However) the basis of everything is its permissibility [wa-l-aṣl ibāḥat al-ašyāʾ].*[40] *(But) he, who might claim that what God has permitted is unlawful shall prove it. However, nothing authentic has been transmitted concerning prohibition or permission. The only certainty is the general rule to which one returns, namely the permission (of all things).*[41]

That nothing authentic has been transmitted about this question is also the opinion of prominent hadith scholars such as Imam aš-Šāfiʿī,[42] Imam al-Buḫarī, Imam an-Nasāʾī, Imam ad-Ḏuhlī, Imam al-Bazzār and Abū ʿAlī an-Nīsāpūrī.[43] But whether or not anal sex is permissible is not the issue of this text. It can be stated that its practice is prohibited according to the main opinion in the four Sunnite schools of law, while the Twelver Shiites regard it permissible.[44] There is a further opinion in the Mālikī school of law, attributed to Imam Ibn al-Qāṣim, Imam Ašhab and Imam Mālik,[45] which classifies it as unpreferable (*makrūh*) but not as prohibited.

In our context here, the focus is rather to point out (**a**) that the Koran addresses sexual practices and (**b**) that the classical scholars were not afraid of talking about them openly and mentioning the arguments of those who had different opinions.

A number of hadith exist beside the Koranic verses, proving that what is perceived as shameful today has no foundation in the sources of Islam. The companions spoke uninhibitedly with the Prophet ﷺ about sexual issues. This can be seen for example in the transmissions for the reason of revelation (*Sabab an-nuzūl*) of Q 2:223.[46]

One transmission illustrating the contrast to our modern age sentiments is the hadith about the wife of Rifāʿa. In one wording of the hadith, narrated by Imam al-Buḫarī, Aischa, the wife of the Prophet, transmits:

> *The wife of Rifāʿa al-Quraẓī came to the messenger of God ﷺ while I was sitting and Abū Bakr was with him. So she said: "O messenger of God, I was together with Rifāʿa and then he divorced me. After my waiting period I married Abdurraḥmān b. az-Zubayr and by God, O messenger of God, his (penis) is like a hem", and thereby she took the hem of her dress. When Ḫālid b. Saʿīd, who waited outside because he had not been let in, heard her statement, he shouted: "Abū Bakr, won't you rebuke her." (But) by God, the messenger of God did only smile (thereupon) and said to her: "Do you want to go back to Rifāʿa? Not before he tasted your sweetness [ʿusaylataki] and you his sweetness [ʿusaylatahu]." From then on this became a Sunna (that means a normative rule).*[47]

Imam al-Buḫarī mentions also another version with further details about this occurrence. It says that her husband was present too, so maybe he arrived after the conversation had started. On her accusation of being impotent, he replied:

> *She is lying, by God, O messenger of God. Truly, I rub her as skin should be rubbed [innī la-anfuḍuhā nafḍa l-adīm].*[48] *But she is tricky and she wants to go back to Rifāʿa.*[49]

This woman, whose name is Tamīma bint Wahb,[50] shows us to our astonishment how self-confident women had been back then. A woman claiming her rights before a judge who – in this case - has been the Prophet ﷺ himself, is no matter of course in many parts of Muslim societies nowadays. A woman, saying in court that her husband does not satisfy her sexual needs is today considered in the category of shameless and obscene. Now the interesting question arises where such categorizations get their justification from. The tradition, and first and foremost the Sunna with its normative function, does not provide any basis for rejecting a behavior which the Prophet ﷺ himself has neither criticized nor corrected. On the contrary, in *uṣūl al-fiqh*[51] the silence of the Prophet is classified as confirmative.[52]

Not only did the Prophet ﷺ remain silent and smile while he listened to Tamīma, but he also explained that she must not remarry her former husband until she had sexual intercourse with her present spouse and then – of course – get divorced. Interestingly, the Prophet did not use a functional term for sexual intercourse but told her: "*Not before he tasted your sweetness ['usaylataki] and you his sweetness ['usaylatahu]*". *'Usayla*, which is a belittlement of *'asal* (honey), serves as a metaphor for sexual encounter.[53] Ibn Manẓūr notes to this part of the hadith: "*He (the Prophet) compared the sexual act with the sweetness of honey and gave it a flavor.*"[54] This is the prophetic sense of shame, which does not make a taboo of certain issues but conveys them in an aesthetic, non-repulsive manner. Moreover, it shall be emphasized that the Prophet ﷺ spoke with this woman about orgasm in the presence of a man who did not belong to her family, namely Imam Abū Bakr, as well as his daughter Aischa. Also the husband's description of how he sexually satisfies his wife: "*Truly, I rub her as skin should be rubbed [innī la-anfuḍuhā nafḍa l-adīm]*", did not irritate the Prophet ﷺ. And neither the Prophet ﷺ, nor the later caliph Abū Bakr رضي الله عنه, respond to the indignation of the Prophet's companion who waited in front of the door.

Today, this companion Ḫālid b. Sa'īd, could be taken as a symbol for the modern-age Muslim, who is influenced by a Victorian sense of shame and modern categories of sexuality. Foucault's description of the pre-Victorian age fits perfectly to the hadith mentioned before: "*Practices were hardly hidden, words were said without exaggerated restraint and things were done without unduly concealing; people lived in familiar and tolerant company with the unseemly.*"[55] This today quite unfamiliar frankness and directness did not only characterize the days of the messenger of God ﷺ but also the lives of Muslims until the late 19th century.[56]

Imam al-Ǧāḥiẓ wrote a fictional debate (*munāẓara*) between a man who sexually preferred young women and another man who preferred lads. The issue of this debate was whether the young lady or the boy offer more pleasure. This text dates back to the 9th century, and al-Ǧāḥiẓ was well aware of the issue's provocative degree; hence he stresses at the beginning of his writing that it is permissible to address such topics for the purpose of entertainment and that it is not blameworthy to call things as they are when it comes to genitals and sexual vocabulary. To give his position a firm basis, he mentioned different stories of the Prophet's companions and the scholars of the first generation. Their statements seem to be forgotten nowadays; therefore, this passage shall get a chance to speak for itself in detail:

> *Some of those who are sanctimonious and show asceticism find it disgusting and show aversion if the vagina, the penis or sexual intercourse is mentioned in front of them. Most of them who behave like this are men who only have as much insight, generosity,*

> *nobleness and manners as they can pretend. Would only one of them know that ʿAbdullah Ibn ʿAbbās*[57] *versified in the Holy Mosque (Mecca) and in the state of ritual purity [muḥrim] these verses:*
>
> *"And they lead us slinking / Were the birds right*[58]*, then I sleep with [nanik] Lamīsa."*[59]
>
> *Thereupon he was told: "But this belongs to rafat̲!"*[60] *He replied: "It is rafat̲ when said in front of women." And would they know the utterance of Ali [....]: "Whose father's penis is long will be invigorated."*[61] *And when it is about (the right understanding of) shamefacedness, Ali is (our) example. [....] and (would they know) what is transmitted about Abū az-Zinād's nephew.*[62] *Because he asked him: "May I moan during copulation?" Abū az-Zinād replied: "Little son, do what you want when you are alone (with your wife)." But the nephew kept on asking: "Uncle, are you moaning too?" He answered: "Little son, if you had seen your uncle during copulation, you would think that I do not believe in God, the Exalted."*[63]

There are lots of similar examples. They show us a drastic change in the understanding of shame and chastity. For Muslims in premodern time, shame was no synonym for tabooing, but rather meant finding the matching words or right conduct in front of a person or in a specific situation (*li-kulli maqām maqāl*).[64] In the normative context however, scholars perceived it as utterly normal to call sex practices or body parts by their names. Thus, Imam al-Qurṭubī wrote in a very open manner about cunnilingus:

> *Asbaġ from our scholars [the Mālikītes] said: "He is allowed to lick her (the vagina) with the tongue [yalḥasahu]."*[65]

The straightforward use of the verb 'lick' in reference to the female genitals in the context of a commentary on the Koran might well be seen as something scandalous today. The shock will be great when the reader realizes that Asbaġ, who made this statement, was a pupil of Imam Mālik and one of the most important scholars of the Mālikī school of law.[66]

And the contemporary reader will be even more amazed when he learns that this uninhibited attitude was common practice. Muǧāhid and Makḥūl for example, two great names among the scholars of the 2nd generation after the Prophet ﷺ, assign the words "*which we have no ability to bear*" in the Koranic verse "*Our Lord, burden us not with that which we have no ability to bear*" Q 2:285 to lustfulness and erection.[67] How many scholars today would have the courage to explain a Koranic verse with such open-mindedness?

One must not think that this open-mindedness could only be found in the legal or exegetic field. Actually, for a long time and maybe until today western research has voyeuristically examined the subject of sex and Islam almost only from the legal normative perspective, evaluating what is prohibited and what is permissible.[68] Hence the next chapter will offer a closer look at those works which address sex and eroticism and will analyze some of their writings by means of examples.

Sex and Eroticism as Subjects

The encyclopedia of science by Imam Ṭāšköprüzāde (d. 1561), *Miftāḥ as-saʿāda* (The key to blessedness), has three entries which directly take up the issue of sex and eroticism: *ʿIlm adāb an-nikāḥ* (Teaching of marital ethics), *ʿilm al-bāh* (Teaching of sex) and *ʿilm al-ġunǧ* (Teaching of erotism). The first entry, located in the chapter about habits (*ādāt*), deals with legal and ethical aspects of marriage and with the wedded life, which also includes sex life.[69] Ṭašköprüzāde assigns the second entry, *ʿilm al-bāh*, to the medical sector which he defines as follows:

> *It is the science which deals with the compounds and nourishments which strengthen sexual power, increase lust, enlarge the penis or narrow the vagina. [....] (It is also a science) which addresses coital positions and habits of the sex act. [....] They (the authors in this field) also mention erotic stories which arouse lust.*[70]

As for *ʿilm al-ġunǧ*, the author places it – interestingly enough – in the domain of musical arts and writes to its definition:

> *It is the teaching referring to the (alluring) activities which come from the young women and beautiful ladies. [....] If the beauty is essential and the play-*

> *fulness natural, it is considered as perfection, but if the playfulness is unnatural, it is one step below perfection. However, everything which originates from beauty is beautiful. [....] This playfulness, if it occurs during the act or while kissing and the like, boosts sexual power. [....] Playfulness is permissible according to the Sharia and women are praised for it in this case (during copulation) and she (the woman) might be rewarded for it (by God) in case of permitted intercourse.*[71]

According to Ṭāšköprüzāde, Muslim scholars at that time were familiar with several teachings and arts dealing with sex. They examined this subject from medical, legal, ethical and sole erotic perspectives as well as the literary perspective.[72] Taking as examples two well-known book catalogs from different periods, the first from the 10th century, which is *al-Fihrist* by Ibn an-Nadīm, and the second from the 17th century, *Kašf aẓ-ẓunūn* by Kâtip Çelebi Ḥāǧǧī Ḫalīfa, we find a list of works which exclusively deal with eroticism and sexual intercourse:

1. *Alfiyya wa-šalfiyya* (One thousand stories)[73]

2. *Kitāb al-bāh* (The book on sex)[74]

3. *Kitāb marṭūs ar-rūmī fī-ḥadīṯ al-bāh* (The book about sex by Marṭūs ar-Rūmī)[75]

4. *Burdān wa-ḥabāḥib*[76]

5. *Kitāb burdān wa-ḥabāḥib aṣ-ṣaġīr* (Burdān wa-ḥabāḥib, the small version)[77]

6. *Kitāb al-ḥurra wa-l-ama* (The free and the maid) as well as *Kitāb as-sāḥiqāt wa al-baġġā'īn* (The lesbians and the indecent)[78]

7. *Kitāb la'ūb ar-ra'īsa wa-ḥusayn al-lūṭī* (On La'ūb the bawd and Ḥusayn the gay)[79]

8. *Kitāb al-ğawārī al-ḥabā'ib* (About the lesbian maids)[80]

9. *Kitāb al-'urs wa-l-'arā'is* (The wedding and the brides)[81]

10. *Kitāb al-qiyān* (The songstresses)[82]

11. *Kitāb al-idāḥ fī-asrār an-nikāḥ* (The revelation of the sexual secrets)[83]

12. *Kitāb al-munākaḥa wa-l-mufātaḥa fī-aṣnāf al-ğimā'* (About sex and its forms)[84]

13. *Kitāb ar-rawḍ al-'āṭir fī nuzhat al-ḫāṭir* (The scented garden)[85]

14. *Kitāb al-faḫḫ al-manṣūb ilā ṣayd al-maḥbūb fī-'ilm al-bāh* (The open trap for hunting the beloved: The teaching of sex)[86]

15. *Kitāb ğāmi' al-laddāt* (The sum of pleasures)[87]

16. *Risāla fī al-bāh wa-asbābih* (Treatise on sex and its reasons)[88]

17. *Kitāb rušd al-labīb ilā muʿāšarat al-ḥabīb* (The conduct of the reasonable during intercourse with the beloved)[89]

18. *Tuḥfat al-ʿarūs* (The guide of the brides)[90]

19. *Dāfiʿ al-humūm wa-rāfiʿ al-ġumūm* (Prevention of afflictions and removal of grief)[91]

20. *Ruǧūʿ aš-šayḫ ilā ṣibāh fī al-quwwah ʿalā al-bāh* (The old man's return to the potency of this youth)[92]

21. *Kitāb al-minhāǧ fī taʿalluqāt al-ilāǧ* (The implications of penetration)[93]

22. *Munyat aš-šubbān fī-muʿāšarat an-niswān* (The desire of the young for intercourse with women)[94]

23. *Nuzhat al-aṣḥāb fī-muʿāšarat al-aḥbāb* (The friends' stroll on the intercourse with the beloved)[95]

24. *Asmāʾ an-nikāḥ* (The names of sexual intercourse)[96]

This list mentions only books from these two catalogs, which were written in Arabic. Certainly more writings explicitly dealing with these issues can be found in the indexes of further works. Similar books have also been published in Ottoman Turkish and Persian, especially in the Indian region with its long tradition of erotic literature. Besides this notable number of sex books, there is a series of works not directly dedicated to the topic of sex but referring to erotic poems, anecdotes or medical advice. Most of the writings about sex and eroticism are actually dispersed among many poetry collections, literal and medical works.[97] In addition to those, we find plenty of love stories so they certainly had been a very popular genre. In his catalogue, Ibn an-Nadīm mentioned one hundred and thirty publications narrating love stories.[98] To our astonishment, the stories are not always about love between a man and a woman but even between men and djinn.[99] The sexual narration has not been subject to normative evaluation but was perceived as a literary genre, received and appreciated from the latter.

Especially those scholars we count among the orthodox camp, have transmitted many erotic anecdotes and stories. Imam ar-Rāġib al-Isfahānī (d. 1108) for example, one of the most famous Koran exegetes, dedicated a whole chapter of more than forty pages to themes like frivolity and lasciviousness, what was said about private parts and coitus, lesbians and lesbianism in his literary compilation *Muḥāḍarāt al-udabā' wa-muḥāwarāt aš-šu'arā'* (The speeches of the cultivated and the conversations of the poets).[100]

Scholars like Imam ar-Rāġib or Imam as-Suyūṭī were not afraid of mentioning stories about homosexuals, lesbians and indecent persons or to describe sexual intercourse in detail, as for them the narration about it belonged to another category than the act itself. Same sex intercourse or extramarital sex is indeed explicitly forbidden according to all four schools of jurisprudence[101] but not so talking about it or taking it as subject of poetry, narrative literature or entertainment. Prior to narrating stories of same sex intercourse,[102] a scholar often had written a few lines about it being prohibited. These few lines are followed by many pages, filled with anecdotes or lyrics about gay people.

The modern reader however, who understands both the act as well as its discourses within the 19th century's creation of 'the sexual', sees a contradiction emerging here. How does it go together that the scholar himself tells us that same sex intercourse or fornication is forbidden and in the same breath fills pages with stories about all sorts of frivolities without any comment? And the modern reader would not only consider the stories by Imam ar-Rāġib, Imam Ibn Kamāl Pascha or Imam as-Suyūṭī part of the erotic domain but in some cases even as pornography and thus characterize or stigmatize them as ideas and concepts alien to Islam, such as 'perverse'.[103] For my part, as a contemporary muslim scholar, I say 'ideas alien to Islam' because the category of 'perverse' needs another category, namely the category of 'normal' to be understood. But what is humanly normal or – to say it in terms of enlightenment – 'natural'? In classic Islam, scholars know five main categories for evaluating human actions.[104] In addition to this, God ﷻ regards humans capable of doing everything. That means, all the things humans do are human and correspond to their abilities and nature, regardless how good or bad their deeds may be *"....and by a soul and Him who formed it, yes induced it sinfulness and piety! Blessed is he who purifies it, unfortunate he who depraved it."* Q 91:7-10. The potential for good or bad is human and from this perspective, all human transgressions are humanly normal. That is the reason why a category like 'perverse' makes no sense from a Koranic point of view.[105] According to the Sunni position, sin is bad only because it is condemned by God but not because of its nature.[106] That is why same sex intercourse and fornication are not regarded as abnormalities or diseases in the classical sense but as transgressions which should be avoided. This differentiation might additionally explain the scholars' frankness in handling these issues. There was nothing perverse in writing such works. Some examples are the story of a woman having sex with a donkey as narrated in Imam ar-Rumi's (d.1273) *al-Mathnawī*[107] or the stories in *Ruǧūʿ aš-šayḫ ilā ṣibāh*[108] by Imam Ibn Kamāl Pascha as well as the unchaste narrations in the collected edition of Imam ar-Rāġib. To learn more about the extent of this lost frankness, some anecdotes mentioned by Imam ar-Rāġib get a chance to be heard:

> *One of the old men [šuyūḫ]*[109] *from Bagdad related: "I called a lad to my chamber and when I was going to penetrate him, the boy said: "Don't do this because I passed my wet hand over my leather socks [ḫuffayn] and I don't want my ritual ablution [wuḍū'] be broken."*[110] *Thereof I learned that rubbing between the thighs does not require major ablution [ġusl] of the two."*[111]

From this passage – and in an even more intense form in some of Imam as-Suyūṭī's writings - we learn that scholars in premodern age had no difficulties to narrate anecdotes, which did not only address forbidden actions but also talk about issues of fiqh with frivolous humor. And, scholars did not only stick to issues of fiqh; they did not spare the Koran either. It should be emphasized once again that the author of the above mentioned anecdote knows the rank of the Koran very well and was among its most famous commentators. Furthermore, he was the author of one of the most important books on ethics.[112] So, we are dealing here with an ethicist and commentator of the Koran. In another section with the title "The boys and women for sale", Imam ar-Rāġib wrote:

> *Abū Nuwās walked by a wreck and saw how an old man mounted a boy; thereat he said: "What are these statues you worship?"* Q 21:52. *The man answered: "We want to eat of these"* Q 5:113. *Then Abū Nuwās replied: "So eat therefrom and feed the needy,*

the poor“ Q 22:28. Then the boy began to speak: “You will not be rewarded until you spend from that which you love“ Q 3:92. [It is also told] that a Koran reciter [muqri’] wanted to seduce a boy. The boy asked him: “What do you give me in exchange?“ He replied: “I will ask pardon for you as long as I live and recite some verses of the Koran for you every day.” The boy rejected, saying: “Rather read for yourself the following verse: And God repelled those who disbelieved in their rage. They did not obtain any good“ Q 33:25. [In another narration it is written] that a man gave some silver coins to a boy. But when the man denuded his penis, the boy became frightened and refused himself. So, the man said: “Either you stand the penetration or you insult Mu‘āwiya.”[113] *The boy replied: ‘‘I prefer the penetration over insulting my uncle*[114] *and commander of the believers.” As he was penetrating him, the boy said: ‘‘O my master! This is little in the love for your friend [waliyy]! O Allah, I sacrificed myself so that Mu‘āwiya will not be vilified, so give me steadfastness.”*[115]

The usage of Koranic passages, however not as Koranic text but rather as elements of normal speech, is a stylistic device in Arabic rhetoric, called *al-iqtibās* or *al-istišhād.*[116] It is generally considered permissible albeit not in joking or frivolous speech.[117] This is at least the position of the majority of the scholars, as Imam aṣ-Suyūtī outlined in a treatise on this subject,[118] which makes this case even more remarkable.

Imam ar-Rāġīb, being a linguist and rhetorician, has surely known the basic rules of citing from the Koran but nevertheless he mentions anecdotes without any comment, which seem to break these guidelines. The least we can note here is that the author did not regard citing these stories, which overstepped a certain limit, as something sinful. These narrations give us insights into society at that time, which was not at all prudish as imagined too willingly by the new representatives of ideologized Islam. Ideal societies never did exist and they never will. Likewise, the attitude of the '*Salaf aṣ-ṣāliḥ*' (the pious ancestors) who are deemed the touchstone of religiosity do not match the Victorian ideas of shame and decency. We read the following statements in another passage of Imam ar-Rāġīb's work:

> *Saʿīd b. al-Musayyib used to say: "O Allah, strengthen my penis for therein lies the satisfaction of my spouse [ahlī]."*[119]
>
> *Ibn Sīrīn said: "The most shameless*[120] *sex is the best." al-Aḥnaf said: "If you want to be loved by women then be shameless in bed and show good manners [with them]." A man asked aš-Šaʿbī: "What do you say if a woman moans [ecstatically] "you kill me, you torture me" during intercourse?" He replied: "He shall kill her [therewith] and her blood money*

is at my expense." [....] It has been said: "One loses his mind in two situations: during copulation and during race."[121]

These statements should not make us think that early Muslims were shameless and libertine. Rather, they show us that shame and decency were related to other ideas and norms and that a drastic change in attitude has happened since then. How we experience that era depends on our own perspective. If modern categories are used, the Muslim society of those days seems immoral, which is actually also – according to Thomas Bauer – the conclusion the western world has drawn.[122] And this conclusion has been adopted by many Muslims. Therewith they faced the dilemma of either overcoming the former perceptions of sex via criticizing and rejecting them or even starting a 'clean- up operation' in their own history. With regard to the latter, this results in an extreme position, which idealizes and ideologizes those early centuries of Islam, so that historically unauthentic images of this era finally come into being. However, such censorship is only possible in those works containing only a few or just partial such 'problematic' chapters.[123]

However, besides literary collections with their numerous provocative stories, there is a particular genre explicitly addressing sex and eroticism. So, the texts of this genre cannot be censored unless these scripts fall into oblivion.

One example of this genre is *Nuzhat al-aṣḥāb fī muʿāšarat al-aḥbāb* by Imam as-Samaw'al b. Yaḥyā (d. 1175).[124] This work originates from a scholar who excels in mathematics, medicine and apology. His book *Nuzhat al-aṣḥāb* consists of two main parts. The first part covers twelve theoretical questions of the sexual life while the second part presents several remedies and addresses various medical questions in twelve chapters. In order to provide an impression of the book's content to readers, it seems useful to me to translate the topics in the first main part.[125]

Chapter 1: The Advantages Of Sex. Chapter 2: The Quantity Of Sex. In this chapter, the author answers the question of how often one needs sex depending on age and physical respectively emotional state. *Chapter 3: About The Reasons Why Some Wish For More And Others For Less Sex. Chapter 4: About Impotence.* Possible medical reasons for invirility, such as cardiac insufficiency or nervous prostration are explained in several sub-chapters. *Chapter 5: Reasons For Aversion To Sex. Chapter 6: About The Deviation From The Natural Way In Sex.* The reasons of same-sex intercourse among men and women is explained in two sub-chapters. Remarkable in this context is the scientificity of the author. He does not regard same-sex intercourse as a disease but rather as something which "*was in wide use among the reasonable in its time*".[126] The fact that something is forbidden in fiqh did not represent an obstacle for examining the forbidden action reasonably with the scientific methods of those times. *Chapter 7: Why Some Young Men Tend To An Unlimited Number Of Pretty Women. Chapter 8: Why The Gnostics Like Sex. Chapter 9: About The Ethics Of Married Life. Chapter 10: On The Purchase Of Slaves. Chapter 11: About Matrimony. Chapter 12: About The Intercession Between Those Wanting To Get Married.*

Another work, treating even more provocative topics, is *Nuzhat al-albāb fī mā lā yūǧad fī kitāb* by Aḥmad b. Yusuf at-Tīfāšī (d. 1253),[127] who was a mineralogist, legal scholar and judge. In twelve chapters he covers stories, anecdotes and poems of various 'deviants'. Even here we find the same scheme: He begins each chapter with mentioning in a few lines the prohibition of this or that practice and then goes on narrating all sorts of uninhibited stories and anecdotes. In some of the chapters he even describes how the dwelling of a *callboy* should ideally look like[128] or how to sneak into somebody's room at night.[129] The reader is faced with a surreal image, which can hardly be brought in line with the common perception of the so called 'Islamic history'[130] or scholarship. By internalizing the fact that this text was written by a judge in the 13th century and that Ottoman Sultan Selim

I read it and had it translated into Ottoman Turkish,[131] many assumptions about Muslim history and the understanding of Islam will be questioned automatically. In short, the book includes the following topics:[132]

Chapter 1: About (Playful) Beating. Chapter 2: About The Ways Of The Pander And The Procuress. Chapter 3: About The Wages And The Attributes Of The Prostitutes. Chapter 4: About The Anecdotes Of The Prostitutes And Their Poems. Chapter 5: About The Anecdotes And Poems Of The Obscene. Chapter 6: About The Wages And Attributes Of The Gays. Chapter 7: About The Anecdotes And Poems Of The Callboys. Chapter 8: About The Anecdotes Of The Gay And Their Poems. Chapter 9: About The Dabb.[133] *Chapter 10: About Anal Intercourse With Women. Chapter 11: About Lesbianism And The Lesbians And Their Anecdotes And Poems. Chapter 12: About The Hermaphrodites And Their Anecdotes And Poems.*

The book *Ruǧūʿ aš-šayḫ ilā ṣibāh* is also ascribed to Imam at-Tifāšī, but some scholars assume the great Ottoman scholar Ibn Kamāl Pascha to be the author. Recent researchers however tend to presume that the original was written by at-Tifāšī but Ibn Kamāl Pascha added on the text and translated it into Ottoman Turkish on the order of Sultans Selim I.[134] This book belongs to the most important works on sex and eroticism and is one of the most comprehensive. It is composed of two parts, one for men and one for women, each comprising thirty chapters. The subjects are very diverse, so there are chapters on anatomy, remedies and medical questions, on the extension of the male genital, on the revitalization of potency, on love, on the things women like during intercourse and on cosmetics. Additionally, the book offers numerous chapters containing erotic stories and anecdotes.[135]

Of course, there are more works[136] but presenting them all would go beyond the scope of this book. That is why the next chapter is limited to the works of Imam aṣ-Ṣuyūṭī.

Finally, it is important to mention that eroticism also played an important role in the writings on *taṣawwuf*. Many poems addressing the beauty of women and the love for them act as allegories for the Sūfi's experiences. In his work *Fuṣūṣ al-ḥikam*, Muḥyī ad-Dīn Ibn al-ʿArabī considers the hadith "Three things from your world have been made lovable to me: women, perfume and prayer" as the essence of the Muḥammadan wisdom and he dedicated the chapter on the Prophet ﷺ to the explanation of this hadith.[137] So, for example, he took the view that divinity can most strongly and most perfectly be perceived in women and this especially during the sexual act.[138] In fact, *taṣawwuf* and eroticism is a broad topic, which I only briefly mention here, in order to show that Muslim scholars have not forgotten eroticism in this domain.

These are some works on the subject: *The Hermeneutics of Eroticism in the Poetry of Rumi* by Mahdi Tourage; *Sufi Narratives of Intimacy: Ibn 'Arabi, Gender and Sexuality* by Sa'diyya Shaikh; *al-Unuṯa fī fikr Ibn 'Arabī* by Nazha Barrada or my essay *Die Weiblichkeit bei Muḥyī ad-Dīn Ibn al-'Arabī* (Femininity in the Writings of Muḥyī ad-Dīn Ibn al-'Arabī).[139]

Imam as-Suyūṭī and his Works on Sex and Eroticism

Imam as-Suyūṭī belongs to those scholars whose works are considered standard references in Koranic studies, *tafsīr*, science of hadith and fiqh. Yet it is not well-known that he has been the Muslim author par excellence in the field of eroticism. Our scholar has indeed written many works which are dedicated directly or indirectly to sexual or erotic themes. In this last chapter we will look into some of his works dealing with these topics.

Unfortunately, research in this area is just at its beginning. Therefore, I found it more fruitful to concentrate on the primary materials in order to obtain an impression of Imam as-Suyūṭī's heritage in the field of eroticism. One of the latest books about Imam as-Suyūṭī was written by George Kadr from Syria, who collected the imam's works on eroticism in three volumes. This is a great convenience for this book as well as for further research, because he includes unpublished manuscripts in his collection. In Kadr's bibliography of Imam as-Suyūṭī's writings we find a lot of works related to issues of sex and eroticism.[140] We will now have a closer look at some of them:

1. *al-Ifṣāḥ fī asmā' an-nikāḥ (The clarity regarding the names of intercourse) and Ḍaw' aṣ-ṣabāḥ fī luġāt an-nikāḥ (The morning light in the linguistic variants of intercourse)*

In these two works, Imam as-Suyūtī discusses the different names and linguistic variations of sexual terms and their meanings. He cites hundreds of names for intercourse, penis, vagina, the noises during sex as well as details of the body. This is mainly a listing of terms with a short linguistic explanation. The same topic can be also found in other texts.

2. *al-Yawāqīt aṯ-ṯamīna fī-ṣifāt as-samīna (The precious pearls in the traits of the corpulent woman)*

Here Imam as-Suyūṭī elaborates on the traits of corpulent women. Two aspects in this work are especially interesting; on the one hand, it shows the contemporary reader the changes in the concepts of beauty; on the other hand, the author gives very detailed descriptions of the bodies of women who actually lived in earlier centuries. Nowadays this would be almost unimaginable for a modern scholar. Imam as-Suyūṭī mentions i.e. 'Ā'iša bint Ṭalḥa,[141] the daughter of one of the most important companions of the Prophet ﷺ in his book with the following description:

> *Ā'iša (bint Ṭalḥa) was well-known for her splendid buttocks. That is why she could not stand upright and she always said: "I am in a misery because of you both (the buttocks)."*[142]

After telling this, Imam as-Suyūṭī does even go one step further and cites the following from older sources:

> *A woman transmitted: "I was at 'Ā'iša bint Ṭalḥa's house and when 'Umar b. 'Abdillāh, her husband (came home), I changed my seat. After he entered, he played with her for a while and then penetrated her [waqa'a 'alayhā]; so she became rampant, moaned and offered a wild performance of movements (rahz) [during intercourse]. After her husband had left, I said to her: "You are of such noble lineage and you enjoy a high social status but nevertheless you behave like this?" She replied: "We do everything for these stallions [fuḥūl] and everything that arises [their lust], so what do you think is wrong with this?" I said: "I prefer such things happen at night." She replied: "It's not like this but rather when he sees me, his lust starts burning, hence he stretches his hand towards me and you have witnessed what happens then."*[143]

Whether or not these narrations are authentic should not be our primary concern here. Because even in cases where such narrations were adulterated and unauthentic, the main question is why Imam as-Suyūṭī and others present such texts. Why didn't he regard giving such detailed descriptions of a woman as well as aspects of her intimate life as violating the rulings of Sharia? The issue of authenticity in this context only raises more questions. The reports remain problematic for the modern reader - no matter how authentic they ultimately are. There are three possibilities: they may be authentic, non-authentic, or the author was not aware of their authenticity. (a) In the case of their being authentic, the question is why the transmitters forward such narrations without hesitation. (b) In the case of their being unauthentic or that Imam as-Suyūṭī and other scholars did not know their status of authenticity, it seems highly problematic from a modern-day perspective. Because, it would mean that the authors narrated things about historical figures that were not true. Yet, due to the overstated modern-age fetishism of historicity, many do not understand that classical scholars were incurious in describing historical incidents. Simply put, many scholars had other intentions when they wrote on topics in *belles-lettres*. The narration itself was the focus, and not the narrative, as the transmission of occurrences, which needed to be authenticated. When this is understood, one comprehends why authenticity was a secondary concern, except in the writing of historiography and normative disciplines, such as fiqh or *kalam*. The transmitted, the narrated and the written had their own dynamics and did not always depend on the historical background of its origin. The text lived by itself and had an end in itself. So, whether or not ʿĀʾiša bint Ṭalḥa was well-known for her splendid buttocks did not matter. The fact is that our imam told this narration in his book, without self-censorship and without feeling ashamed. The Salafi or the ideologist, thinking in modern-age categories, would probably try to deny the authenticity of these narratives. However, he cannot deny the fact that these texts can be found in numerous works of Muslims scholars in the premodern age.

3. Nuzhat al-ʿumr fī-tafḍīl al-bīḍ wa-sūd wa-sumr (The comparison between white-skinned, black and brown women)

This treatise is a collection of several poems, dealing with the question of whether white-skinned, black or brown women are more beautiful. To answer this question, Imam as-Suyūṭī presents four opinions: the opinions of those who prefer one group and the opinions of those who are just respectively undecided. The poems include subtle erotic images describing the beloved who is sometimes a male and sometimes a woman.[144]

4. Nuzhat al-ǧulasāʾ fī ašʿār an-nisāʾ (The poems of the women)

The book is a collection of biographical anecdotes and poems of popular Arab women. The poems deal with love and desire and also with sex. I regard female poetry as the most important source for studies on the daily life of women in premodern Muslim societies, as well as, for obtaining insights into women's emotions and sorrows in those days. Especially the fragments, spread here and there mostly in poems, anecdotes and biographies, allow us a rough reconstruction of the "world of women" in premodern Muslim societies, but not the normative texts, which generally talk about a desired condition of society instead of its actual status quo. Imam as-Suyūṭī's collection of narrations is authentic concerning this matter. He does not censor but rather just cites the poems and anecdotes exactly as narrated in older scripts. He also quotes the most lascivious anecdotes from these scripts without criticism. Two examples illustrate his calm attitude. The first one is taken from Wallāda bint al-Mustakfī, to which Imam as-Suyūṭī writes:

> *With golden threads she stitched the following verse on the right side of one of her dresses:*
>
> *'Truly I am qualified for the noble/ And in my course is insobriety'*[145]

and on the left side:

> *'I bestow my cheek to the beloved / A kiss I give the one who desires it.'*[146]

The second example originates from another poetess, Ṯawāb bint ʿAbdillāh al-Ḥanẓaliyya. Imam as-Suyūṭī mentioned that a man wanted to marry her; her reply were the following verses:

> *Your penis has no hope at the door of my vagina / Dispel him from the door of my vagina and lead him to where he came from.*[147]

After this verse, Imam as-Suyūṭī cites the well-known lexicographer and writer Abū Manṣūr aṯ-Ṯaʿālibī (d. 1038) without any criticism:

> *By God, with these two verses she became more well-known than Kabša bint ʿAmr, Ḫansāʾ bint Ṣaḫr, Ǧanūb al-Huḏayliyya and Laylā al-Uḫayliyya.*[148]

How many theologians today would publicly declare their admiration for similar poems? Even today's scholars, whom we assume to be committed to tradition, and to have a solid education in traditional knowledge, may themselves think in categories which have little in common with tradition. A concealed apologetics directed against an absent audience can often be found in their attitudes and positions. Many of those who are perceived as classical scholars represent only images of scholarliness of the late 19th and early 20th century and in no way an unaffected authentic tradition, because most of them would be at a loss as to how to react or would react defensively and negatively to such texts by previous scholars.

5. al-Mustaẓraf fī aḫbār al-ǧawārī (The anecdotes of the maids)

This book is similar to the previous one with the sole difference being that it focuses on maids. The text includes poems and anecdotes with an erotic touch.[149]

6. al-Mustaḍrafa fī duḫūl al-ḥašafa (About the penetration with the glans)

The work belongs to the field of fiqh and discusses the legal consequences of penetrating the vagina with the glans. Consequences include for example invalidating the fast[150] or the pilgrimage but also the maturity of the complete dowry after the marriage contract.[151] Imam as-Suyūṭī mentions about 150 legal consequences in total from all fields of law. It needs to be emphasized that this treatise is not a comment on a poem of Ibn al-ʻAfīf, as Ḥāǧǧ ī Ḫalīfa states in his index. This is a mistake as George Kadr ascertained after he had examined and edited the manuscript of *al-Mustaḍrafa fī duḫūl al-ḥašafa*, which is available in the al-Asad Library.[152]

7. al-Wišāḥ fī fawā'id an-nikāḥ (About the benefit of sex)

Here we deal with a summary of an unpublished work of the imam, which is divided in three main chapters. The first chapter is a collection of transmissions of the Prophet ﷺ, the companions and the early scholars who address the subject of sex in many facets. The intention here is to show that sex is something recommended, good and praiseworthy if carried out lawfully. The second chapter addresses more than 400 synonyms for the term *ǧimāʿ* which means sexual intercourse, sex or coitus.[153] Occasionally he explains synonyms to differentiate them from one another, as they are not always identical synonyms but rather terms with slight lexicographical nuances. Furthermore, he presents hundreds of synonyms in Arabic for the terms penis, glans, vagina and its sections as well as for the movements during intercourse. The third chapter is a collection of erotic anecdotes.

8. Šaqā'iq al-utruǧ fī raqā'iq al-ġunǧ (The subtleties in eroticism)

In this essay, Imam as-Suyūṭī addresses the women's art of seduction. The text is a response to the question whether *ġunǧ*[154] is permissible for women. *Ġunǧ* is not just seduction in general but is inseparably connected with sexual seduction and a lack of restraint.[155] Here, the text gives us clear evidence that Muslims understood the sexual act not only as an act of procreation but more likely as a pleasure for both partners. And because it is something enjoyable, the seductive, erotic and, yes, even the shameless does play an important role in it. Imam as-Suyūṭī starts the text with a linguistic essay in which he explains some of the terms in detail, including *ar-rafaṯ*, meaning the desirous talking during intercourse or the act itself,[156] or *ar-rahz* which has several meanings, as for example stimulating motions during sex but also pillow talk.[157]

9. Nawāḍir al-ayk fī ma'rifat an-nayk (About sex)

Nawāḍir al-ayk fī-ma'rifat an-nayk can be counted among the boldest books on this subject, next to *Rašf az-zulāl min as-siḥr al-ḥalāl* (The sweet drops in permissible magic), as this work of Imam as-Suyūṭī covers only sexual issues. Central subjects are the sexual positions and motions. Imam as-Suyūṭī specifies over a hundred and forty sex positions in this book. In his study, George Kadr came to the amount of two hundred positions, when corresponding notes in other works of the great imam are also taken into account.[158] These are significantly more than in the classical book Kama Sutra, which talks about 64 positions.[159] Besides the sex positions, Imam as-Suyūṭī addresses sexual desire in general in this work, but also topics like the female ejaculation, the female sexual desire and the motions during intercourse. Numerous anecdotes and poems are added by him, which nowadays hardly anybody would expect from a scholar like Imam as-Suyūṭī. But this discrepancy is only rooted in today's way of thinking and not in the texts of the imam. It is important to give some examples of the anecdotes he mentioned in this work, in order to provide an idea of this lost frankness.

> *Abū al-Ǧamūs al-Bazzāz narrated: "When I was still young, I went to the house of Ḥamdūna b. ar-Rašīd with my teacher to sell a precious silken dress. It was Daqqāq*[160] *who negotiated the price with us in a frivolous way in front of the door. She held a fan in her hand on which was written: The vagina does rather need two penises than the penis needs two vaginas just like the mill rather needs two mules than a mule needs to mills."*[161]

In another narration mentioned by him, we read:

> *It was narrated that when a grammarian wanted to make love to his wife, he told her: "Come here, press your back against the floor, stretch your legs heavenwards, receive the penis with your vagina and moisten it with biṣāq (saliva) and if you want with bisāq and if you want with bizāq, as all have the same meaning just like the (Koranic readings) ṣirāṭ (way), sirāt and zirāt." Hardly had he finished his statement when his wife threw herself on the ground. Her husband asked: "What are you doing?" She replied: "I thank God that I was allowed to experience how three interpretations are read on my vagina."*[162]

The usage of theological terminology or generally professional terminology of other disciplines like grammar or rhetoric to describe erotic scenes can be found in many poems and narrations as seen earlier in the example of the anecdote between Abū Nuwās and the old man; but, no scholar has mastered it the same way as Imam as-Suyūṭī. He devoted a complete book to this genre, namely:

10. Rašf az-zulāl min as-siḥr al-ḥalāl (The sweet drops in permissible magic)

This work belongs to the genre of *maqāmat*, which are rhymed prose texts. In his *maqāma*, Imam as-Suyūṭī narrates the fictive story of twenty scholars who prayed the Eid prayer together. During the Eid sermon, the imam mentioned the advantages of marriage and of sexual intercourse as the term *nikāḥ* has both meanings. After the sermon, all twenty friends decided to marry the same day. And in fact, they all got married the same day. Besides the fact of how quickly they wedded, the story seems quite normal. The next day, the brothers of hearts came together and each one had to describe the first night with his wife or - more precisely - each one had to unveil how intercourse with his spouse had been.[163] So, the author let each of the twenty scholars describe his wedding night within the terminology of his own subject. Imam as-Suyūṭī mastered the ability to visualize the sexual act by means of linguistic games and ambiguous terms from different disciplines. Based on these twenty reports, one notes how the religious, as well as the linguistic terminology is eroticized in the Arabic language. Two passages shall illustrate this. We read in the report of the scholar of hadith:

> *...qālat: taḥtāǧ ilā tamhīd al-maslak*[a] *fa-aḫadtu fī-l-irsāl*[b] *wa-l-waqf*[c] *wa-l-idrāǧ*[d]*...*[164]

[a]: she said: "*You need to smooth the way.*" The word *tamhīd* indicates a well-known commentary of the hadith collection *al-Muwaṭṭa'*.

[b]: *So, I started to send (him)*; *al-irsāl* literally means 'to send' but in the science of hadith it is a techni-

cal term for a transmission in which the name of the companion, who had listened directly from the Prophet ﷺ, is not mentioned.

[c]: *and to stop*; *al-waqf* means that the chain of transmission goes back to a companion, but not back unto the Prophet ﷺ himself.

[d]: *and to insert*; the meaning of *al-idrāğ* is to insert a word or a sentence into the transmitted.

The second passage originates from the description of the jurist. Here we read:

> *wa-sawwaktu taġra al-farğ bi-siwāki al-īr mutaladdidan*[a] *[...] wa-nawaytu al-i'tikāf*[b][165]

[a]: *And I have 'petted' the orifice of the vagina with my penis*. Imam as-Suyūṭī made use of the verb *sawwaka*, which means cleaning the mouth with the miswāk.[166] The brushing of the teeth itself is a recommended act before prayer, therefore the verb *sawwaka* is used by the jurist.

[b]: *and I intended to dwell*. For the word 'dwelling' - indicating the lingering of the penis in the vagina - Imam as-Suyūṭī used the word *i'tikāf*, which in fiqh means the retreat in the mosque for the purpose of praying and remembrance of God.

The author masters to show the fluidity of language in this artwork of ambiguity. He demonstrates how to picture erotic moments and images by using religious and 'sacralized' terminology. He thereby questions our modern sacrality, which we have attributed to this terminology and maybe he even questions our entire modern-age understanding of Islam. Such linguistic tools make us aware of the banality of categories such as religious or sacred, and we realize how the modern secularization of language has sometimes ironically caused a sacralization of things which had never been sacred in tradition.

Epilogue

The aim of this book is to raise questions within the theological and historical field.

Why was it possible for scholars like al-Isfahānī, Ibn al-ʿArabī or as-Suyūṭī to write about certain things with a frankness and directness, which seems so unfamiliar to us nowadays? What has caused the taboo around certain issues and genres? And why did censorship start with scholars deemed sophisticated and contemporary like Muḥammad ʿAbduh?[167] This change in attitude raises many questions and further researches will be necessary to obtain a clearer understanding about the developments of the last two hundred years. We learned that for Muslims the concept of theology includes issues which hardly are expected in theology in its occidental form. We also learned that themes such as the enjoyment of instincts, the advantages of sexual intercourse, sex positions, and the description of the woman have been discussed in commentaries of the Koran and hadith, in the works of *taṣawwuf* and fiqh. A Christian theologian in premodern time and even today probably would not be expected to write Kama Sutra-like books to achieve God's good will.

Another point I tried to emphasize is the necessity to distinguish between normative literature and historical reality. What is written in normative works does not directly represent people's everyday experiences during the past centuries, nor does it show how Islam was understood in the practical sense. As soon as literature, history and other genres, such as fatwa collections are taken into consideration, it becomes apparent that the life of Muslims did not always correspond to the alleged normative ideas. The thinking of premodern scholars was characterized by pragmatics and not, like today, by obsessive efforts to establish ideals which had never existed...

God and His Prophet know it best
and peace and blessings upon
him who was sent as
a mercy upon
the worlds.

Appendix I

An erotic description of the Kaaba: From Tāǧ ar-rasāʾil (The crown of the epistles)[168] *by Muḥyī ad-Dīn Ibn al-ʿArabī (d. 1240)*

Praise be to God, He who bestowed upon me the crown of honor after devotion, He who dressed me with the vesture of majesty after walking humbly, He who brought me together with the unique virgin among the entities, who neither man nor an invisible being had deflowered. And peace and blessings as long as day and night exist upon the chosen master of the house of ʿAdnān.

Now, after God سبحانه وتعالى had led me to His sanctuary, showed me His holy house and brought me together with the Kaaba, the delightful beauty, who equals an umbrageous blossoming garden, I beheld a divine being, an angelic-like reality, a transcendental young woman of royal origin and Meccan manners.[169]

Simultaneously I saw a hanging veil, a hand, which is kissed, and words, which are heard. Yemenite and Syrian breezes came [her] way.

I experienced an embracing, a caressing, a sucking of mouth nectar and a passionate embrace. Eloquent is her playfulness and adored is her boldness.

Enormous is her beauty and unsurpassable her majesty. She is unfaded beauty; yes, a rarity is she. Her forehead shines and her nose is straight.

Her size is perfect, her cheek gentle. She is a pleasure garden protected from the sun. She is not bored and she does not bore. Her eyes are heavenly big and she struts and seduces with her sides.

A white with a flat belly
with shining breasts like a mirror

Her teeth are like pearls, her breath like the essence of musk, her fingers delicate and her eyelids temptingly swollen, her scent is amber. Ever cheerful is she, patient, standing upright; and, she knows neither rejection nor turning away.

She cures after she hurt.

Her speech is sweet and her mouth delicious. Her seduction is gentle, her guidance severe. She afflicts, she is a companion of sleeplessness, she enchains the thoughts, she enchants the beholders, she makes the bodies melt and extinguishes the souls. She thins the bodies and glows inside and brings there embers. She disciplines the desires. However, she keeps her promises because she is faithful. Divine is her origin, glorious is her descent, spiritual is her reality, and comforting her sight.

Had you heard her speech, you would say she is an eloquent Arab.

Had you seen her latent hints, you would say she is a silent Syrian.

Her description complies with three names, with which Baššār b. Burd[170] has pictured his beloved:

A virgin maid, unified in her
a branch, a hill and a moon

That means she is upright like a branch, her precious buttocks equal a hill and her eyes are like moonlight

And I mentioned also a fourth virtue in one of my rare poems:

A full moon covered by rain clouds
rises above a tenuous twig
standing on a selected sandhill

Thus, I have added comparing seduction with the darkness of night to the description. Her seduction is humiliating. She is unique in her ages, unprecedented in her epoch, unequalled in her time. Her subtlety is indescribable.

She is a sun above the seven skies. Gabriel dwelt with her, Abraham, the friend of God, leaned against her and the Exalted praised her.

I gave her a sign and laid my hand on hers and so we held conversations and we extolled the eternal and the created while people circumambulated us and the yearning lingered in front of her door.

However, she and I were under a cover, which the others did not notice. We had intimate conversations and dialogs which included spiritual insights, divine mysteries, *muḥammadan* beverages and unified latent hints.

Between noon and afternoon and after she had fettered me with the secret of time, she ordered me to instantly put down in a booklet my latent hints I had told her. So, I did what she commanded. I did not transgress her ruling, the spiritual conversations we had, nor the divine breath of the glorious presence.

The servants' messengers of divine names imparted the correspondence between us and they conveyed my wish for complete oneness with the high and low station until universality occurs and until the hidden secret becomes clear.

So, I wrote in this booklet pieces of what my spiritual state and my capacity allowed me to. For truly, the undertaking is enormous, the thoughts are weak, the beloved is tired, the lover faint, the heart on fire and it burns throughout the whole body.

So be modest, oh inquirer, with what my pencil has delivered on the paper because that is what I can bear.

God is my help and Him I trust.

Appendix II

About pleasure and beauty: Excerpts from the book I'tilāl al-qulūb (The visitation of the hearts) by al-Ḥāfiẓ al-Ḫarā'iṭī (d. 937)

Ibn 'Awn narrated: An old woman told us: "I seek refuge with God from the lustfulness of the old men."[171]

Makḥūl said regarding the Koranic passage 'Our Lord, do not impose upon us a duty beyond our scope' Q 2:285: "This refers to lustfulness."[172]

'Abdullāh b. Ṣāliḥ narrated: When al-Layṯ b. Sa'd wanted intercourse, he secluded himself in a room of his house and had himself brought a cloth which was worn these days and was called *al-Burkān*. When he withdrew, he used to say the following: "O Allah, let it [the penis] get hard, raise its chest and smooth for it the doorway and exit. Bestow its lust on me and grant me progeny who fight for Your cause." He ['Abdullāh b. Ṣāliḥ] added: al-Layṯ had a loud voice so that one could hear this invocation of him.[173]

The father of 'Imāra b. Waṯīma narrated: 'Abdullāh b. Rabī'a was among the most decent and chaste of the Qurayš. But his penis never found rest so that he never participated in good nor bad events. And whenever he married a woman from the Qurayš, she stayed only a few days with him before she fled back to her family. Regarding this, Zaynab, the daughter of ʿUmar, son of Abū Salama, asked: "Why do they flee from their cousin [this means member of their clan]?" She was told: "They cannot bear him [sexually]." She replied: "What keeps him [from marrying me] as I am the one with the sublime character traits and with the superb buttocks and the gorgeous vagina." The narrator added: So he married her and she could take him and she gave birth to six sons.[174]

Ibn Sirīn narrated that a woman complained about her husband to Anas b. Mālik because she could not bear him [sexually]. So [Anas] judged that he must not have intercourse with her more than six times a day and night.[175]

Ḫālid al-Ḥadd̲ ā' related that when Adam had intercourse with Eve, she said to him: "O Adam, this is delightful, give us more thereof."[176]

ʿAbdullāh b. Šawdab narrated: A beautiful woman came to al-Ḥasan al-Baṣrī and asked him: "Tell me, O Aba Saʿīd, may a man take another woman next to his wife?" He said: "Sure!" She replied: "Even next to such a woman?" and she unveiled her face which did not equal any other face in beauty and continued: "O Aba Saʿīd, don't give men such legal consultations (fatwa)", and went away. al-Ḥasan said: "A man who has such a woman at home should not care about this world any more."[177] [This means, he should not be interested in other women.]

Abū al-Ḥassan al-Madā'inī related: One day 'Imrān b. Ḥiṭṭān, who was ugly, disgusting and small, came to an admirable woman who had made herself beautiful for this purpose. When he saw her, she seemed even more beautiful to him and he admired her for a long time. Thereupon she asked him what was wrong with him. He replied: "By God, you are indeed entrancing." She said: "Then let me bring you the glad tidings that we both will be in paradise." He asked her: "How do you know that?" She replied: "Because you found someone like me and are grateful; and, I was haunted by someone like you and show forbearance, [and as you know] the thankful and the patient are both in paradise."[178]

Notes

1 AS-SUYŪṬĪ, ĞALĀL AD-DĪN: *al-Wišāḥ fī fawā'id an-nikāḥ*, Damaskus: Dār al-kitāb al-'arabī n. d., p. 33.

2 The adjective 'Islamic' is used quite often to state a phenomenon's affiliation with Islam. The Arabic term itself however is a neologism. Moreover, the category 'Islamic' is one of modernity's inventions and for me, it seems to be misleading, not only because it has no equivalent in tradition, but also because it gives the impression of an absolute parameter by which the 'Islamness' of phenomena can be categorized. For this reason, I avoid the usage of this adjective. Here it has been merely mentioned to expose these problems.

3 Fiqh is often translated as science of deducing norms or jurisprudence. Within the theological tradition, both the normative research of the divine tidings (*waḥy*) as well as its results are called fiqh.

4 "*at-Taṣawwuf is the science which explores the inner dimension of Islam. The aim is pure realization by purification of the soul according to the norms of Sharia.*" GHANDOUR, ALI: *Fiqh. Einführung in die islamische Normenlehre*, Freiburg im Breisgau: Kalam Verlag 2015, p. 80.

5 See AS-SUYŪṬĪ, ĞALĀL AD-DĪN: *ad-Durr al-manṯūr*, Kairo: Dār hāğar 2003, vol X, p. 198.

6 http://en.wikipedia.org/wiki/Abdel-Bari_Zamzami (accessed June, 26th, 2014).

7 Imam al-Ḥasan al-Baṣrī was one of the most popular scholars of Baṣra and among the best-known ascetics of

the 2nd generation after the Prophet.

8 Muslims in those days knew sex toys, as documented e.g. by Imam Ibn al-Qayyim. In his book *Badāi' al-fawā'd* (The excellent usage information) he describes a kind of dildo made of leather, which women in those days used for sexual stimulation and he transmitted the view of some Ḥanbalītes who regarded the usage as permissible even though he did not tend to this position. See IBN QAYYIM AL-ǦAWZIYYA, MUḤAMMAD: *Badā'i' al-fawā'id*, Mekka: Maktabat nizār nuṣtafā al-bāz 1996, vol. IV, p. 905.

9 Cf. IBN ḤAZM, 'ALĪ: *al-Muḥallā*, Kairo: Dārat aṭ-ṭibā'a al-munīriyya 1352, vol. XI, p. 390.

10 Cf. ibid., vol. XI, pp. 390 ff.

11 See BAUER, THOMAS: *Die Kultur der Ambiguität*: eine andere Geschichte des Islams, Berlin: Verlag der Weltreligionen 2011, pp. 268–311.

12 Cf. ibid., p. 270.

13 Cf. ibid., p. 273.

14 Cf. FOUCAULT, MICHEL: *Der Wille zum Wissen. Die Hauptwerke*, 3rd ed., Frankfurt: Suhrkamp Verlag 2008, p. 1070.

15 *"Sharia in some way expresses the entirety of the divine tidings. However, it is no statute book and even less a synonym for penal law as sometimes understood wrongly today. The Sharia is not codified in the form of laws nor is it written down at all; the Sharia is beyond the letters of the alphabet and, as Rüdiger Lohlker states, "not in its totality knowable by man". [...] The Sharia is timeless and divine. Thomas Bauer writes: "Sharia first of all means the divine judgements of human actions." As the Sharia is something divine and as it is not accessible by man in its entirety, nobody can say of*

himself to possess it or be able to comprehend it. From a theological perspective, it is something, which only the divine knowledge and the divine will can comprehend and which inheres the divine tidings (waḥy). It represents the Absolute, which can only be approximately conceived and understood. We no longer do talk about Sharia but about fiqh, when e.g. rules or norms are derived from the Sharia as a revealed and proclaimed divine message or order." GHANDOUR, ALI: *Fiqh. Einführung in die islamische Normenlehre*, Freiburg im Breisgau: Kalam Verlag 2015, p. 18.

16 Cf. PARRINDER, GEOFFREY: *Sexualität in den Religionen der Welt*, Düsseldorf: Patmos 2004, p. 267.

17 Cf. NIETZSCHE, FRIEDRICH: *Der Antichrist*, Hamburg: Nikol 2008, p. 133.

18 *Sunan an-Nasāʾī*: vol. 36, ch. 1 (print version of Thesaurus Islamicus Foundation, Vaduz 2001).

19 Cf. SCHÖLLER, MARCO, AL-NAWAWI UND IBN DAQIQ AL-'ID: *Das Buch der Vierzig hadithe. Kitab al-Arba'in*. With the comment of Ibn Daqiq al-'Id, 2nd ed., Frankfurt am Main: Verlag der Weltreligionen im Insel Verlag 2007, p. 166.

20 Imam Ǧaʿfar aṣ-Ṣādiq (d. 765) is a descendant of Imam al-Hussain, the grandson of the Prophet. He is considered an authority in multiple theological disciplines particularly in fiqh and teachings of tradition. He plays a central role for both Sunnis and Shiites. For the latter he is the 6th of the 12 Imams.

21 AL-ʿĀMILĪ, MUḤAMMAD B. ḤASSAN: *Tafṣīl wasāʾil aš-šīʿa ilā taḥṣīl masāʾil aš-šarīʿa*, Qom: Muʾassasat Āl al-bayt li-iḥyāʾ at-Turāṯ 1414, vol. XX, p. 22.

22 Ibid.

23 Faḫr ad-Dīn ar-Rāzī was a theologian, jurist and Koran

exegete. His works in the field of *tafsīr* (Koran exegesis), *kalām* (systematic theology) and *uṣūl al-fiqh* (methodology of the science of deducing norms) are considered standard references until today.

24 Cf. AR-RĀZĪ, FAḪR AD-DĪN: *at-Tafsīr al-kabīr*, Beirut: Dār al-fikr 1981, vol. XXIX, pp. 129 f.

25 Ibid., vol. XXXI, p. 21.

26 Cf. IBN QAYYIM AL-ĞAWZIYYA, MUḤAMMAD: *Ḥādīal-arwāḥ ilā bilād al-afrāḥ*, Jeddah: Dār ʿālam al-fawāʾid 1428, p. 482.

27 Cf. ibid., p 473.

28 He was a prominent scholar of the Hanbalīte school of law and a loyal follower of the scholar Ibn Taymiyya.

29 IBN QAYYIM AL-ĞAWZIYYA: *Ḥādī al-arwāḥ ilā bilād al-afrāḥ*, p. 476.

30 Cf. AL-QURTUBĪ, ABŪ ʿABDILLĀH : *al -Ğāmiʿ li-aḥkām al-qurʾān*, Beirut: Muʾassasat ar-risāla 2006, vol. XX, p. 199.

31 Cf. AL-ĀMIDĪ, SAYF AD-DĪN: *Abkār al-afkār fī-ʿilm al-kalām*, Kairo: Dār al-kutub wa-l-watāʾiq al-qawmiyya 2004, vol. IV, pp. 261 ff.

32 See i.e. the explanation of Q 2:223 from aš-Šanqīṭī (d. 1974), a scholar who was influenced by Wahhabite Islam. AŠ-ŠANQĪṬĪ, MUḤAMMAD AL-AMĪN: *Aḍwāʾ al-bayān fī-iḍāḥ al-qurʾān bi-l-qurʾān*, Beirut: Dār al-fikr 1995, pp. 92 ff.

33 A Hanbalīte scholar from Jerusalem and autor of one of the comprehensive encyclopedias of fiqh (science of deducing norms).

34 IBN QUDĀMA, MUWAFFAQ AD-DĪN: *al-Muġnī*, Beirut:

Dār al-fikr 1405, vol. VIII, p. 132.

35 He was a legal scholar and Koran commentator from Andalusia. Till today, his Koran commentary is regarded as one of the primary sources of Koranic exegesis.

36 Cf. QURTUBĪ: *al-Ğāmiʿ li-aḥkām al-qurʾān*, vol. IV, p. 7.

37 Cf. ibid., vol. IV, p. 8. All three came from Medina and were among the most important scholars of the 2nd generation after the Prophet. Saʿīd b. al-Musayyib in particular had a special status. He is called the crown of scholarship of his time.

38 Imam Abū Bakr Ibn al-ʿArabī al-Maʿāfirī from Andalusia is a central figure of the Mālikī school of law. He is known for his numerous commentaries of the Koran and of important hadith collections such as i.e. *al-Muwaṭṭaʾ* or *Sunan at-Tirmiḏī*.

39 IBN AL-ʿARABĪ, ABŪ BAKR: *Aḥkām al-qurʾān*, Beirut: al-Maktaba al-ʿaṣriyya 2003, vol. I, p. 198.

40 This means, all things and actions are permissible in principle until the opposite is proven in the sources of the Sharia.

41 IBN AL-ʿARABĪ, MUḤYĪ AD-DĪN: *ʿAğāʾib al-ʿirfān*, Beirut: Dār al-kutub al-ʿilmiyya 2007, p. 257.

42 See AN-NAWAWĪ, ŠARAF AD-DĪN: *al-Mağmūʿ šarḥ al-muhaḏḏab, Dschidda*: Maktabat al-iršād, vol. XVIII, p. 103.

43 Cf. al-ʿASQALĀNĪ, IBN ḤAĞAR: *Fatḥ al-bārī*, Beirut: Dār al-kutub al-ʿilmiyya 2002, vol. II, p. 695.

44 For the Shiite position see AN-NAĞAFĪ, MUḤAMMAD ḤASSAN: *Ğawāhir al-kalām fī-šarḥ šarāʾiʿ al-islam*, Beirut: Dār

Iḥyā' at-turāṯ al-'arabī 1981, vol. XXIX, p. 103.

45 See AL-ḤAṬṬĀB, AR-RU'AYNĪ : *Mawāhib al -ġalīl šarḥ muḫtaṣar ḫalīl,* Beirut: Dār al-kutub al-'ilmiyya 1995, vol. V, p. 24 f.

46 See AṬ-ṬABARĪ, ABŪ ǦA'FAR: *Tafsīr aṭ-ṭabarī,* Kairo: Dār hağar 2001, vol. III, pp. 754 ff.

47 *Ṣaḥīḥ al-Buḫārī*: vol. 77, ch. 6 (print edition of Dār al-minhāğ, Dschidda, 1429)

48 This is an illustration of energetic intercourse.

49 Ibid., vol. 77, ch. 23.

50 Cf. IBN 'ABD AL-BARR, ABŪ 'UMAR: *al-Istiḏkār,* Damaskus: Dār qubba li-ṭ-ṭibbā'a 1993, vol. XVI, p. 153.

51 Methodology of the science of deducing norms.

52 See AL-ĠAZĀLĪ, ABŪ ḤĀMID: *al-Mustaṣfā min 'ilm al-uṣūl,* Damaskus: ar-Risāla al-'ilmiyya 2012, vol. 2, p. 231.

53 Cf. Ibn Manẓūr, Ǧamāl ad-Dīn: Lisān al-'arab, Beirut: Dār al-ma'ārif 1998, p. 2946.

54 Ibid.

55 FOUCAULT: *Der Wille zum Wissen,* p. 1029.

56 Cf. BAUER: *Kultur der Ambiguität,* p. 290.

57 The cousin of the Prophet.

58 This could also be translated as "*would my intuition be right*".

59 An Arabic female name.

60 *Rafaṯ* means intercourse, intimacy as well as pillow talk.

61 In this proverb, the length of the penis is a metaphor for virility. That means, if the father was potent, the probability that he will have a number of sons, who will support each other, is high.

62 One of the prominent scholars of Medina and teacher of Imam Mālik. See his biography in AḎ-ḎAHABĪ, ŠAMS AD-DĪN: *Siyar aʿlām an-nubalāʾ*, Beirut: Muʿassasat ar-risāla 1996, vol. V, pp. 445 ff.

63 AL-ǦĀḤIẒ, ABŪ ʿUṮMĀN: *Rasāʾil al-ǧāḥiẓ*, Kairo: Maktabat al-ḫānuǧī 1964, vol. II, pp. 92 ff.

64 Ibid., vol. II, p. 93.

65 QURTUBĪ: *al-Ǧāmiʿu li-aḥkām al-qurʾān*, vol. XV, p. 217.

66 See his biography in: AḎ-ḎAHABĪ: *Siyar aʿlām an-nubalā*ʾ, vol. X, pp. 656 ff; see also AZ-ZIRIKLĪ, ḪAYR AD-DĪN: *al-Aʿlām*, Beirut: Dār al-ʿilm li al-malāyīn 2002, vol. I, p. 333.

67 Cf. AS-SĀʿĀTĪ, MUḤAMMAD RĀǦĪ: *Rašf ar-riḍāb wa fākihat al-aḥbāb*, Beirut: Atlas 2013, p. 36.

68 Cf. BAUER: *Die Kultur der Ambiguität*, p. 279.; see also PARRINDER: *Sexualität in den Religionen der Welt*, pp. 186–217.

69 Cf. *Ṭāšköprüzāde, Aḥmad*: *Miftāḥ as-saʿāda*, Beirut: Dār al-kutub al-ʿilmiyya 1985, vol. III, pp. 196 ff.

70 Ibid., vol. I, pp. 326 f.

71 Ibid., vol. I, p. 377.

72 Cf. Bauer: Kultur der Ambiguität, pp. 284 ff.

73 Cf. AN-NAǦAFĪ, MUḤAMMAD ḤASSAN: *Ǧawāhir al kalām fi-šarḥ šarāʾiʿ al-islām*, Beirut: Dār iḥyāʾ at-turāṯ al-

ʿarabī 1981, vol. I, p. 157.

74 Cf. Ibn an-Nadīm, Muḥammad b. Isḥāq: *al-Fihrist*, Beirut: Dār al-maʿrifa 1978, p. 243.

75 Cf. ibid., p. 436

76 Cf. ibid., the two names appear in later texts in different variants, i.e. *Barraǧān*, *Burraǧān* or *Ḥubāhib*.

77 Cf. ibid.

78 Cf. ibid.

79 Cf. ibid.

80 Cf. ibid.

81 Cf. Ḥāǧǧ ī Ḫalīfa, Muṣṭafā: *Kašf aẓ-ẓunūn*, Baghdad: Maktabat al-muṯannā 1941, vol. II, p. 1438.

82 Cf. ibid., vol. II, p.1451.

83 See aš-Širāzī, ʿAbd ar-Raḥmān: *al-Idāḥ fī-asrār an-nikāḥ*, (Vollers Ms. 0775 -01), Universitätsbibliothek Leipzig 1507; cf. Ḥāǧǧ ī Ḫalīfa: *Kašf aẓ-ẓunūn*, vol. I, p. 209.

84 Cf. Ḥāǧǧ ī Ḫalīfa: *Kašf aẓ-ẓunūn*, vol. II, p. 1845.

85 Nafzâwî und Ulrich Marzolph: *Der duftende Garten: Ein arabisches Liebeshandbuch*, 1st ed., München: C.H. Beck Verlag 2002.

86 Cf. Ḥāǧǧ ī Ḫalīfa: *Kašf aẓ-ẓunūn*, vol. II, p. 1241.

87 Cf. ibid., vol. I, p. 571.

88 Cf. ibid., vol. I, p. 850.

89 Cf. az-Ziriklī, Ḫayr ad-Dīn: *al-Aʿlām*, Beirut: Dār al-ʿilm li-l-malāyīn 2002, vol. I, p. 203; see also Ḥāǧǧ ī

Ḫalīfa: *Kašf aẓ-ẓunūn*, vol. I, p. 904.

90 Cf. Ḥāǧǧ ī Ḫalīfa: *Kašf aẓ-ẓunūn*, vol. I, p. 370.

91 Cf. ibid., vol. I, p. 729.

92 Cf. ibid., vol. I, p. 835.

93 Cf. ibid., vol. II, p. 1877.

94 Cf. ibid., vol. II, p. 1885.

95 Cf. ibid., vol. II, p. 1940.

96 Cf. ibid., vol. I, p. 81.

97 Some examples are *al-Aġānī* by Abū al-Faraǧ al-Isfahānī, *'Uyūn al-aḫbār* by Ibn Qutayba or *Muḥāḍarāt al-udabā'* by ar-Rāġib al-Isfahānī.

98 Cf. Ibn an-Nadīm: *al-Fihrist*, pp. 425 ff.

99 Cf. ibid., pp. 327 f.

100 See al-Isfahānī, ar-Rāġib: *Muḥāḍarāt al-udabā' wa-muḥāwarāt aš-šu'arā'*, Beirut: Maktabat al-ḥayāt 1960, vol. II, pp. 242–280.

101 Several scholars transmitted the consensus that same sex intercourse is explicitly prohibited; see i.e. Ibn Ḥazm, 'Alī: *Marātib al-iǧmā'*, Kairo: Dār al-muslim 2010, p. 297. The prohibition refers to the sexual act itself; the category of homosexuality is unknown in tradition. Same sex love or the admiration of one's own sex's beauty as a social phenomenon or literary genre was widely accepted among Muslims until the adoption of the categories of homosexuality formed in the western world. For more details on this point as well as how Muslims experienced the transformation in thinking concerning this topic, see Bauer: *Die Kultur der Ambiguität*, pp. 268 ff.

102 See i.e. AL-ISFAHĀNĪ: *Muḥāḍarāt al-udabāʾ wa-muḥāwarāt aš-šuʿarāʾ*, vol. II, p. 242.

103 Cf. BAUER: *Die Kultur der Ambiguität*, pp. 284 ff.

104 These are: permissible, obligatory, prohibited, recommended, undesirable. See: AL-ĠAZĀLĪ, ABŪ ḤĀMID: *al-Mustaṣfā min ʿilm al-uṣūl*, Damaskus: ar-Risāla al-ʿilmiyya 2012, vol. I, p. 127.

105 Interesting is also the change in terminology. In pre-modern age, homosexuality was referred to as '*al-liwāṭa*', a quite neutral term, which characterized the people of Lot. In the modern age, this term was dismissed and replaced by a neologism from the western discourse on sexuality in psychology, which is '*aš-Šuḏūḏ al-ǧinsī*' (the sexual abnormality). The idea of homosexuality being a disease has no basis in tradition. According to the classical schools of law, same sex intercourse is a forbidden action but not an illness, as defined in psychology for a long time.

106 Cf. AL-ĠAZĀLĪ: *al-Mustaṣfā*, vol. I, pp. 112 f.

107 See RUMI, JELALADDIN: *Das Masnavi*, Herrliberg: Edition Shershir 2012, vol. V, pp. 98–103.

108 See IBN KAMĀL PASCHA, AḤMAD: *Ruǧūʿaš-šayḫ ilā ṣibāh fī al-quwwati ʿalā al-bāh*, Kairo: Būlāq 1309 A.H, pp. 90–92.

109 The expression '*Šayḫ*' is ambiguous because it means scholar as well as old man.

110 *Wuḍūʾ* means the minor ablution; some schools of law allow to pass over leather socks or shoes with wet hands instead of washing the feet. However, they should be put off if one needs to wash the entire body. As penetration requires major ablution and the boy would have to put off

his leather socks, he did not want the penetration.

111 AL-ISFAHĀNĪ: *Muḥāḍarāt al-udabā' wa-muḥāwarāt aš-šu'arā'*, vol. II, pp. 250 f.

112 These works are "*aḏ-Ḏarī'a ilā makārim aš-šarī'a*" (The shari'ite character traits) and "*al-Aḫlāq*" (Ethics). Cf. AZ-ZIRIKLĪ: *al-A'lām*, vol. II, p. 255.

113 Here, *Mu'āwiya b. Abī Sufyān* is meant; he is a companion of the messenger of God.

114 *Mu'āwiya b. Abī Sufyān* has the title "uncle of the believers".

115 AL-ISFAHĀNĪ: *Muḥāḍarāt al-udabā' wa-muḥāwarāt aš-šu'arā'*, vol. II, pp. 246 f.

116 AṢ-ṢUYŪṬĪ, ĞALĀL AD-DĪN: "*Raf' al-bās wa-kašf al-iltibās fī ḍarb al-maṯal min al-qur'ān wa-l-iqtibās*", in: *al-Ḥāwī li-l-Fatāwī*, vol. II, Beirut: al-Maktaba al-'aṣriyya 1990, p. 400.

117 Cf. ibid., p. 431.

118 See ibid., pp. 399-441.

119 AL-ISFAHĀNĪ: *Muḥāḍarāt al-udabā' wa-muḥāwarāt aš-šu'arā'*, vol. II, p. 270.

120 In the original Arabic text, the superlative '*afḥašuhu*' is used which does not only mean 'most shameless' but also 'most uninhibited', 'most frivolous'. In modern Arabic, this term could actually be translated as 'most perverse'.

121 AL-ISFAHĀNĪ: *muḥāḍarāt al-udabā' wa-muḥāwarāt aš-šu'arā'*, vol. II, p. 266.

122 See BAUER: *Die Kultur der Ambiguität*, pp. 295, 305.

123 Cf. ibid., pp. 302 f.

124 A manuscript has been used for this article: Ibn Yaḥyā, as-Samaw'al: *Nuzhat al-aṣḥāb fī-mu'āšarat al-aḥbāb* (Vollers 0774), Leipzig University Library's 1507.

125 The complete index can be found at the beginning of the manuscript; see ibid., fol. 3-6.

126 Ibid., fol. 21, rear side.

127 at-Tīfāšī, Aḥmad b. Yusuf: *Nuzhat al-albāb fī mā lā yūğad fī kitāb*, London: Riyyad al-rayyes Books 1992.

128 Cf. ibid., p. 141.

129 Cf. ibid., p. 209.

130 The term 'Islamic history' as well as all modern constructs, composed of the adjective 'Islamic', are misleading as history is beyond religion. History does include elements of religion and has been influenced by it but nevertheless it remains history. One can only talk about geographically limited areas in limited periods of time. The Great Narrative of Islamic history which claims to be the alleged homogeneous fourteen hundreds of years old history of an area between western Africa and eastern China should be abandoned in modern research.

131 Cf. Ḥāğğ ī Ḫalīfa: *Kašf aẓ-ẓunūn*, vol. I, p. 835.

132 See at-Tīfāšī: *Nuzhat al-albāb fī mā lā yūğad fī kitāb*, pp. 9–10.

133 *ad-Dabb* means that a person tiptoes to somebody's room to have sexual intercourse while others are in the house.

134 Cf. as-Sā'ātī, Muḥammad Rāğī: *Rašf ar-riḍāb wa fākihat al-aḥbāb*, Beirut: Atlas 2013, pp. 13 ff.

135 See IBN KAMĀL PASCHA: *Ruǧūʿ aš-šayḫ ilā ṣibāh fī al-quwwah ʿalā al-bāh*, pp. 3, 45 f.

136 Like i.e. *Tuḥfat al-ʿarūs* by Muḥammad at-Tīǧānī or *ar-Rawḍ al-ʿāṭir fī-nuzhat al-ḫāṭir* by an-Nafzāwī, which has been translated into German by Ulrich Marzolph.

137 Cf. IBN AL-ʿARABĪ, MUḤYĪ AD-DĪN: *Fuṣūṣ al-ḥikam*, Beirut: Dār al-kitāb al-ʿarabī 2002, pp. 214 ff.

138 Cf. ibid., p.217.

139 See www.ibnarabi.de

140 For the detailed list of works as well as their different editions and manuscripts, see Kadr, George: *Fann an-nikāḥ fī-turāṯ šayḫ al-islām ǧalāl ad-dīn as-suyūṭī*, Beirut: Atlas Books 2011, vol. I, pp. 30 ff.

141 See her detailed biography in IBN ʿASĀKIR, ABŪ AL-QĀSIM: *Tārīḫ Dimašq*, Beirut: Dār al-fikr 1998, vol. LXIX, pp. 249-260.

142 KADR: *Fann an-nikāḥ fī-turāṯ šayḫ al-islām ǧalāl ad-dīn as-suyūṭī*, vol. II, p. 150.

143 Ibid.

144 See i.e. AS-SUYŪṬĪ, ǦALĀL AD-DĪN: *Nuzhat al-ʿumr fī tafḍīl al-bīḍ wa-s-sūd wa-s-sumr*, Kairo: Maktabat at-turāṯ al-islāmī 1987, pp. 22, 29, 34.

145 KADR: *Fann an-nikāḥ fī-turāṯ šayḫ al-islām ǧalāl ad-dīn as-suyūṭī*, vol. III, p. 250.

146 Ibid.

147 Ibid., vol. III, p. 257.

148 Ibid.

149 See i.e. ibid., vol II, pp. 83 f, p. 133.

150 Cf. ibid., vol I, pp. 275 f.

151 Cf. ibid., vol I, p. 278.

152 See ibid., vol I, p. 273.

153 See AS-SUYŪṬĪ, ĞALĀL AD-DĪN: *al-Wišāḥ fī fawā'id an-nikāḥ*, Damaskus: Dār al-kitāb al-'arabī n. d., pp. 91 ff.

154 Depending on its context, this term may be translated as erotic seduction or eroticism.

155 See AS-SUYŪṬĪ, ĞALĀL AD-DĪN: *Rašf az-zulāl min as-siḥr al-ḥalāl*, Beirut: Mu'assasat al-instišār 1997, pp. 63 ff.

156 Cf. ibid., pp. 65 f.

157 Cf. ibid., p. 68.

158 Cf. KADR: *Fann an-nikāḥ fī-turāṯ šayḫ al-islām ğalāl ad-dīn as-suyūṭī*, vol. I, pp. 172 f.

159 Richard Burton: The Kama Sutra of Vatsyayana (see bibliography).

160 Daqqāq was a female singer who studied with the famous singers of the Abbasid Empire. She was well-known for her beauty, facetiousness, frivolity and chivalry. For her biography see AL-ISFAHĀNĪ, ABŪ AL-FARAĞ: *al-Aġānī*, Beirut: Dār ṣadir 2008, vol. XII, p. 203.

161 AS-SUYŪṬĪ, ĞALĀL AD-DĪN: *Nawāḍir al-ayk fī-ma'rifat an-nayk*, Damaskus: Dār al-kitāb al-'arabī n. d., p. 37.

162 Ibid., p. 108

163 See AS-SUYŪṬĪ: *Rašf az-zulāl min as-siḥr al-ḥalāl*, pp. 15 ff.

164 Ibid., p. 34.

165 Ibid., p. 47.

166 A bud or a piece of root from a toothbrush tree (Salvadora persica), which was used for brushing the teeth.

167 My colleague Florian Lützen informed me that when Gernot Rotter edited *Maqāmāt al-Hamadānī*, he noted that Muḥammad ʿAbduh had removed a *maqāma* as well as other passages from his edition because he regarded their wording as too obscene. Cf. AL-HAMADHANI UND GERNOT ROTTER: *Vernunft ist nichts als Narretei. Die Maqamen*, (Bibliothek arabischer Erzähler), München: Goldmann Wilhelm GmbH 1990, p. 20.

168 IBN AL-ʿARABĪ, MUḤYĪ AD-DĪN: "*Tāǧ ar-rasāʾil wa-minhāǧ al-wasāʾil*", in: ʿAbda al-Fattāḥ, Saʿīd (ed.): *Rasāʾil Ibn ʿArabi* (2), Beirut: Muʾassasat al-instišār 2002, pp. 237–240.

169 Here, the Šayḫ is describing his vision in wakefulness, which he experienced during circumambulating the Kaaba. He wrote about this occurrence in chapter 72 of *al-Futūḥāt al-makkiyya*. According to his narration, the Kaaba initially was angry with him, because he never mentioned her high stations. After an event in which she manifested herself as a beautiful but wrathful virgin, he recited a poem in front of her, which she enjoyed. This was the beginning of a relationship and conversations between her and Šayḫ al-Akbar, which he wrote down in the book *Tāǧ ar-rasāʾil*. The text at hand is a translation of its prologue. See IBN AL-ʿARABĪ, MUḤYĪ AD-DĪN: *al-Futūḥāt al-Makkiyya*, Kairo: Dār al-Kutub al-ʿarabīyya 1911, vol. 1, pp. 700 f.

170 Baššār b. Burd al-ʿUqaylī was one of the well-known Arab poets of the second century after Hegira. He died in Baṣra in the year 784. See AZ-ZIRIKLĪ, ḪAYR AD-DĪN: *al-Aʿlām*, Beirut: Dār al-ʿIlm li-l-malāyīn 2002, vol. II, p. 53.

171 AL-ḪARĀʾIṬĪ, MUḤAMMAD B. ǦAʿFAR : *Iʿtilāl al-qulūb*, Mekka: Maktabat nizār nuṣtafā al-bāz 2000, p. 105.

172 Ibid.

173 Ibid., p. 106.

174 Ibid.

175 Ibid., pp. 106 f.

176 Ibid., p. 107.

177 Ibid., p. 147.

178 Ibid., pp. 153 f.

Bibliography

AL-ĀMIDĪ, SAYF AD-DĪN: *Abkār al-afkār fī 'ilm al-kalām*, Kairo: Dār al-Kutub wa-l-Watā'iq al-Qawmiyya 2004.

al-'ĀMILĪ, MUḤAMMAD B. ḤASSAN: *Tafṣīl wasā'il aš-šī'a ilā taḥṣīl masā'il aš-šarī'a*, Qom: Mu'assasat āl al-bayt li-iḥyā' at-turāṯ 1414.

AL-'ASQALĀNĪ, IBN ḤAĞAR: *Fatḥ al-bārī*, Beirut: Dār al-kutub al-'ilmiyya 2002.

BAUER, THOMAS: *Die Kultur der Ambiguität: eine andere Geschichte des Islams*, Berlin: Verlag der Weltreligionen 2011.

AL-BUḪĀRĪ, MUḤAMMAD B. ISMA-'ĪL: *Ṣaḥīḥ al-Buḫārī*, Dschidda: Dār al-Minhāğ 1429.

AḎ-ḎAHABĪ, ŠAMS AD-DĪN: *Siyar a'lām an-nubalā'*, Beirut: Mu'assasat ar-risāla 1996.

FOUCAULT, MICHEL: *„Der Wille zum Wissen"*, Die Hauptwerke, 3. Aufl., Frankfurt: Suhrkamp Verlag 2008.

AL-ĞĀḤIẒ, ABŪ 'UṮMĀN: *Rasā'il al-Ğāḥiẓ*, Kairo: Maktabat al-ḫānuğī 1964.

AL-ĠAZĀLĪ, ABŪ ḤĀMID: *al-Mustaṣfā min 'ilm al-uṣūl*, Damaskus: ar-Risāla al-'ilmiyya 2012.

GHANDOUR, ALI: *Fiqh: Einführung in die islamische Normenlehre*, Freiburg im Breisgau: Kalam Verlag 2015.

ḤĀĞĞĪ ḪALĪFA, MUṢṬAFĀ: *Kašf aẓ-ẓunūn*, Baghdad: Maktabat al-muṯannā 1941.

AL-ḪARĀ'IṬĪ, MUḤAMMAD B. ĞA'FAR: *I'tilāl al-qulūb*, Mekka: Maktabat nizār muṣṭafā al-Bāz 2000.

al-Ḥaṭṭāb, ar-Ru‘aynī: *Mawāhib al-ǧalīl šarḥ muḫtaṣar ḫalīl*, Beirut: Dār al-kutub al-‘ilmiyya 1995.

al-Hamadhani und Gernot Rotter: *Vernunft ist nichts als Narretei. Die Maqamen. (Bibliothek arabischer Erzähler).*, München: Goldmann Wilhelm GmbH 1990.

Ibn ‘Abd al-Barr, Abū ‘Umar: *al-Istiḏkār*, Damaskus: Dār Qubba li-ṭ-ṭibbā‘a 1993.

Ibn al-‘Arabī, Abū Bakr: *Aḥkām al-qur'ān*, Beirut: al-Maktaba al-‘aṣriyya 2003.

Ibn al-‘Arabī, Muḥyī ad-Dīn: *al-Futūḥāt al-Makkiyya*, Kairo: Dār al-kutub al-‘arabīyya 1911.

Ibn al-‘Arabī, Muḥyī ad-Dīn: *Fuṣūṣ al-ḥikam*, Beirut: Dār al-kitāb al-‘arabī 2002.

Ibn al-‘Arabī, Muḥyī ad-Dīn: *„Tāǧ ar-rasā'il wa-minhāǧ al-wasā'il“*, in: ‘Abda al-Fattāḥ, Sa‘īd (Hrsg.): *Rasā'il Ibn 'Arabi* (2), Beirut: Mu'assasat al-instišār 2002.

Ibn al-‘Arabī, Muḥyī ad-Dīn: *'Aǧā'ib al-'irfān*, Beirut: Dār al-kutub al-‘ilmiyya 2007.

Ibn ‘Asākir, Abū al-Qāsim: *Tārīḫ dimašq*, Beirut: Dār al-fikr 1998.

Ibn Ḥazm, ‘Alī: *al-Muḥallā*, Kairo: Dārat aṭ-ṭibā‘a al-munīriyya 1352.

Ibn Ḥazm, ‘Alī: *Marātib al-iǧmā'*, Kairo: Dār al-muslim 2010.

Ibn Kamāl Pascha, Aḥmad: *Ruǧū'aš-šayḫ ilā ṣibāh fī al-quwwati 'alā al-bāh*, Kairo: Būlāq 1309H.

Ibn Manẓūr, Ǧamāl ad-Dīn: *Lisān al-'urub*, Beirut: Dār al-ma‘ārif 1998.

IBN AN-NADĪM, MUḤAMMAD B. ISḤĀQ: *al-Fihrist,* Beirut: Dār al-maʿrifa 1978.

IBN QAYYIM AL-ĞAWZIYYA, MUḤAMMAD: *Badāʾiʿ al-fawāʾid,* Mekka: Maktabat nizār muṣtafā al-bāz 1996.

IBN QAYYIM AL-ĞAWZIYYA, MUḤAMMAD: *Ḥādī al-arwāḥ ilā bilād al-afrāḥ,* Dschidda: Dār ʿālam al-fawāʾid 1428.

IBN QUDĀMA, MUWAFFAQ AD-DĪN: *al-Muġnī,* Beirut: Dār al-fikr 1405.

al-ISFAHĀNĪ, ABŪ AL-FARAĞ: *al-Aġānī,* Beirut: Dār ṣadir 2008.

AL-ISFAHĀNĪ, AR-RĀĠIB: *Muḥāḍarāt al-udabāʾ wa-muḥāwarāt aš-šuʿarāʾ,* Beirut: Maktabat al-ḥayāt 1960.

KADR, GEORGE: *Fann an-nikāḥ fī-turāṯ šayḫ al-islām ğalāl ad-dīn as-ṣuyūṭī,* Beirut: Atlas Books 2011.

NAFZÂWÎ UND ULRICH MARZOLPH: *Der duftende Garten: Ein arabisches Liebeshandbuch,* 1. Aufl., München: C.H. Beck Verlag 2002.

AN-NAĞAFĪ, MUḤAMMAD ḤASSAN: *Ğawāhir al-kalām fī-šarḥ šarāʾiʿ al-islām,* Beirut: Dār Iḥyāʾ at-turāṯ al-ʿarabī 1981.

AN-NASĀʾĪ, ABŪ ʿABD AR-RAḤMĀN: *Sunan an-Nasāʾī,* Vaduz: Thesaurus Islamicus Foundation, 2001.

AN-NAWAWĪ, ŠARAF AD-DĪN: *al-Mağmūʿ šarḥ al-muhaḏḏab,* Dschidda: Maktabat al-iršād.

NIETZSCHE, FRIEDRICH: *Der Antichrist,* Hamburg: Nikol 2008.

PARRINDER, GEOFFREY: *Sexualität in den Religionen der Welt,* Düsseldorf: Patmos.

AL-QURTUBĪ, ABŪ ʿABDILLĀH: *al-Ğāmiʿ li-aḥkām al-qurʾān,* Beirut: Muʾassasat ar-risāla 2006.

AR-RĀZĪ, FAḪR AD-DĪN: *at-Tafsīr al-kabīr,* Beirut: Dār al-fikr 1981.

RICHARD BURTON: *The Kama Sutra of Vatsyayana,* http://www.gutenberg.org/files/27827/27827-h/27827-h.htm. (Juli 2015)

RUMI, JELALADDIN: *Das Masnavi: Buch 5,* Herrliberg: Edition Shershir 2012.

AŠ-ŠANQĪṬĪ, MUḤAMMAD AL-AMĪN: *Aḍwā' al-bayān fī-iḍāḥ al-qur'ān bi-l- qur'ān,* Beirut: Dār al-fikr 1995.

AS-SĀ'ĀTĪ, MUḤAMMAD RĀĞĪ: *Rašf ar-riḍāb wa fākihat al-aḥbāb,* Beirut: Atlas 2013.

SCHÖLLER, MARCO, AL-NAWAWI UND DAQIQ AL-'ID: *Das Buch der Vierzig hadithe: Kitab al-Arba'in. Mit dem Kommentar von Ibn Daqiq al-'Id,* 2. Aufl., Frankfurt am Main: Verlag der Weltreligionen im Insel Verlag 2007.

AS-SUYŪṬĪ, ĞALĀL AD-DĪN: *ad-Durr al-manṯūr,* Kairo: Dār hāğar 2003.

AS-SUYŪṬĪ, ĞALĀL AD-DĪN: *al-Wišāḥ fī-Fawā'id an-nikāḥ,* Damaskus: Dār al-Kitāb al-'arabī o. J.

AS-SUYŪṬĪ, ĞALĀL AD-DĪN: *Nawāḍir al-ayk fī-ma'rifat an-nayk,* Damaskus: Dār al-kitāb al-'arabī o. J.

AS-SUYŪṬĪ, ĞALĀL AD-DĪN: *Nuzhat al-'umr fī-tafḍīl al-biḍ wa-sūd wa-sumr,* Kairo: Maktabat at-turāṯ al-islāmī 1987.

AṢ-ṢUYŪṬĪ, ĞALĀL AD-DĪN: *„Raf' al-bās wa-kašf al-iltibās fī-ḍarb al-maṯal min al-qur'ān wa-l-iqtibās",* in: *al-Ḥāwī li-l-fatāwī* Bd. II, Beirut: al-Maktaba al-'Aṣriyya 1990.

AS-SUYŪṬĪ, ĞALĀL AD-DĪN: *Rašf az-zulāl min as-siḥr al-ḥalāl,* Beirut: Mu'assasat al-instišār 1997.

ṬĀŠKÖPRÜZĀDE, AḤMAD: *Miftāḥ as-sa'āda*, Beirut: Dār al-kutub al-'ilmiyya 1985.

AṬ-ṬABARĪ, ABŪ ǦA'FAR: *Tafsīr aṭ-ṭabarī*, Kairo: Dār hağar 2001.

AT-TĪFĀŠĪ, AḤMAD B. YUSUF: *Nuzhat al-albāb fī mā lā yūǧad fī kitāb*, London: Riyyad al-Rayyes Books 1992.

AZ-ZIRIKLĪ, ḪAYR AD-DĪN: *al-A'lām*, Beirut: Dār al-'ilm li-l-malāyīn 2002.

Manuscripts

IBN YAḤYĀ, AS-SAMAW'AL: *Nuzhat al-aṣḥāb fī-mu'āšarat al-aḥbāb* (Vollers Ms. 0774), Leipzig: Universitätsbibliothek Leipzig 1507.

AS-SUYŪṬĪ, ǦALĀL AD-DĪN: *al-Wišāḥ fī-fawā'id an-nikāḥ* (Ms. 1199; Sg. Aḥmad Ḫayrī), Mekka: Umm al-Qurā University 1176 n. H.

List of Eulogies

سبحانه وتعالى Praise be upon Him (God)

ﷺ Peace and blessings be upon him (The messenger of God)

رضي الله عنه May God be pleased with him (mainly for the companions of the Prophet)

Index

A

B

C

D

E

F

G

H

I

K

L

M

Memos

Memos

About the Autor

Ali Ghandour studied oriental studies and political science at the University of Leipzig and completed his PhD in Islamic theology (Theological Epistemology of Muḥyī ad-Dīn Ibn al-ʿArabī) at the University of Münster. He has published an introduction to fiqh and an annotated translation of Abū Ḥānifa's al-fiqh al-akbar.

www.ingramcontent.com/pod-product-compliance
Lightning Source LLC
Chambersburg PA
CBHW020325130626
46549CB00003B/1028
* 9 7 8 3 9 8 1 7 5 5 1 4 5 *